ROAD TO THE UPPER ROOM

A Narrative of the Last Months, Week, and Day of Jesus

Dennis Doughty

21st Century Christian

ISBN: 978-0-89098-537-3
eISBN: 978-0-89098-960-9

©2013 by 21st Century Christian
2809 12th Ave S, Nashville, TN 37204
All rights reserved.

All rights reserved. No part of this publication may be reproduced, stored in a retrieval system, or transmitted in any form or by any means—electronic, mechanical, photocopy, recording, digital, or otherwise—without the written permission of the publisher.

Unless otherwise noted Scripture quotations are from the New American Standard Bible.
Scripture taken from the NEW AMERICAN STANDARD BIBLE®,
Copyright © 1960,1962,1963,1968,1971,1972,1973,1975,1977,1995 by The Lockman Foundation. Used by permission.

Scripture quotations marked NEB are from the New English Bible.
Scripture quotations taken from the New English Bible, copyright © Cambridge University Press and Oxford University Press 1961, 1970. All rights reserved.

Scripture quotations marked NIV are from the New International Version.
Scripture quotations taken from THE HOLY BIBLE, NEW INTERNATIONAL VERSION®, NIV®
Copyright © 1973, 1978, 1984, 2011 by Biblica, Inc.™ Used by permission. All rights reserved worldwide.

The "NIV" and "New International Version" trademarks are registered in the United States Patent and Trademark Office by Biblica. Use of either trademark requires the permission of Biblica US, Inc.

Cover design by Jonathan Edelhuber, with Matthew Cleveland
Illustrations by Matthew Cleveland

Dedication:
I dedicate this book to my Mother,
Eva Jane Doughty.
She is one of the greatest women I have ever known
and she somehow raised both of her children to become writers.
I love you, Mom.

Table of Contents

The Narrative:
Section One - The Last Months

An Evil Darkness 13
The Feast of Dedication 17
Bethany Beyond the Jordan 23
"Lazarus Is Sick" 29
Return to Bethany 35
"Lazarus Come Forth" 41
The Plot to Kill 47
Ephraim and Galilee 55
Return to Jerusalem 63

Section Two - The Last Week

The City of Palms 71
"Zaccheus, Come Down" 77
From Jericho to Bethany 83
Anointed for Burial 89
Sunday's Triumphal Entry 95
Cleansing the Temple, Again 103
Monday's Quiet Day 109
Tuesday's Confrontations 117
The Final Teachings 127
In Caiaphas' Courtyard 133

Section Three - The Last Day

Thirty Pieces of Silver 139
Peter and John Make Ready 147
The Upper Room 153
Judas and the Sop 161
The Bread and the Cup 167
"Let Not Your Heart Be Troubled" 173
Out to Gethsemane 177
Epilogue 183

Section Four - The Lessons

Review Section 1 – The Last Months 191
Review Section 2 - The Last Week 193
Review Section 3 - The Last Day 195
Christ's Greatest Miracle 197
The Fruitless Fig Tree 203
A Pound of Perfume 207
Judas the Betrayer 211
The Bread and the Body 215
The Cup and the Blood 219
Jesus' After Dinner Speeches 223
The Failings of the Pharisees 227
A Cup of Tea at Calvary 231

Introduction

The great old gospel hymn proclaims; "Tell me the story of Jesus, write on my heart every word; Tell me the story most precious, Sweetest that ever was heard." The goal of this book is simply to to tell the story of Jesus; to tell of his last months, his last week, and his last day up on this earth.

While serving as Chaplain for a medical missions group in Guatemala, I first begin to tell this story. Our group of 20 Christians was spending a couple of days in Antigua at the end of our mission trip. On Saturday evening I arranged for an empty conference room at our hotel and assembled our group. There, while everyone sat on the floor, I told the story of Jesus in the Upper Room. I had been studying this material for a year. For the next two years I continued to study this theme and develop the material. During this time I had several more opportunities to tell the story, often upon request. On each occasion I was impressed with the response I received. I realized that most of us have never really pieced together the last months and moments of Jesus life as it happened.

So for the duration of this material I will not be a preacher or a teacher. I will be a storyteller. I'm going to tell a part of "the greatest story ever told;" a very important part! I want to tell it in a way it has not been told before; at least I have never heard it or read it this way in my fifty years as a Christian. I want to tell it to you in a chronological narrative format.

Any casual Bible student has realized that the gospels were not written in precise chronological order. Matthew, Mark, Luke, and John each wrote with their own special approach, with their own unique memories, and under the revealing, inspiring, and sometimes limiting direction of the Holy Spirit (2 Peter 1:21). The Spirit wanted us to see the teaching, power and the divinity of Christ. He was not trying to produce a screen play. John, Luke, Mark and Matthew were not writing their memoires, nor as it turns out, a biography of Jesus of Nazareth. The commentator William Henriksen states; "in fact writing a biography of Jesus was not at all their purpose... any attempt to construct a perfect 'Harmony' so that at a glance one can see exactly what order the various events occurred, is doomed to failure."

Therefore, it takes some effort for us to piece a lot of things together if we want to look at the events is a chronological story format. Having said this, much of the chronology is there, it is just that the Holy Spirit scattered bits and pieces of it throughout the four gospel accounts. I have tried to construct it together using the timeline of the scriptures as well as other background information, geography, archeology, secular writings and at times my own feel for the moment.

I will not claim that in trying to put the pieces of this sometimes complex puzzle together that my chronology is flawless, but it is well studied. There are other historical accounts, such as the writings of Josephus, which give us a better understanding of some events. Yes, I have had to read between the lines some to help the story flow. I trust my "reading" is close to the mark. In some ways my two visits to Israel and Jerusalem helped me to "visualize" the events, and at least to better understand the geography and culture of the land.

Introduction

I pray that this unique approach will help the story come alive to you. Maybe reading it in this way will help you to better envision this great period of the Lord upon this earth, and in so doing your faith will be strengthened. I began this study to help me focus better upon the Lord's Supper as I partook of it each week. It has made my weekly remembrance of our Lord's sacrifice much more meaningful. Perhaps it will do the same for you.

I want to thank my nephew, Matthew Cleveland, for helping me tell this story by his wonderful illustrations. I remember him as a kid always drawing his comic book characters, and as a teenager he used his art talent in church VBS's and other Bible class events. When I asked him about illustrating this book, I did not know if his talent was really up to the task, that is until I saw his first few drawings! His contribution to this work adds to its unique approach.

The emphasis of this story concerns the last travels and last week of Jesus, and the events of the Upper Room in particular. I realized many years ago that the gospel writers gave a great deal of attention to this last week. Put together as a whole, thirty-five percent of the four gospels are spent on Christ's last week. Fifty percent of the gospel of John is centered on these last few days. It is an important week, and a time period where we have a great deal of information about what is happening.

The gospel writers and the Holy Spirit are telling us that this week is of great importance! But do we ever stop and look at it as the dramatic spellbinding story that it is? Let us do so now.

Dennis Doughty

The Narrative

Section One:
The Last Months

Chapter One
An Evil Darkness

> *"At the sixth hour darkness came over the whole land until the ninth hour."*
> Mark 15:33

It was dark in the city of Jerusalem. It was quiet, and it was dark. It was not the beautiful darkness of a moonlit night, casting soft shadows across rolling hills. It was not the darkness that comes at midnight upon a city nestled under a starry sky in the rest of peaceful sleep. This was an evil darkness which had come upon a busy city at noonday. The people of this city had committed such a horrific deed upon an innocent man that the sun's Creator had refused to let it shine upon the event. It was a darkness that smelled of death, and so black that hardened soldiers shook in fear[1] and women wept[2]. It was the darkness that comes upon a

1 Matthew 27:54
2 Luke 23:27; Matthew 27:55,56

place when God abandons it. Only the Prince of Darkness moved about, pleased by the events that took place around a rocky hillside outside Jerusalem.

On this hillside there stood three crosses. On either side hung two rightfully-punished, and self-professed thieves. The center cross was a different story. God's son hung there. Deity had become flesh; omnipotence had become pierceable. His brow was blooded from the crown of thorns that dug into his scalp. Helplessly he hung there, the muscles of his outstretched arms quivering from the pain and trauma suffered by six long hours of stretching and tearing. His breathing was labored. His body, for hours racked in pain, had now become cold and numb. As his eyes opened for a moment, he saw the blur of torches in the darkness and heard the voices of the Roman soldiers beneath him. God's Son made one final effort to draw some air into his lungs, as it escaped he whispered, "It is finished," and the earth beneath the cross began to shake.

True, this death brought us life. His crucifixion took away our condemnation. His suffering brought our salvation. But why this horrible, bloody scene? How did it come to this? How did God's Son, who came to experience life as a man, become so rejected?[3] Through the womb of a woman[4], this Son of Man who chose to enter this world as we all have. He chose to live under the same law he helped install at Sinai[5]. How could he be the man on the center cross? This lover of children, and healer of the sick, this good son and skillful carpenter - how could they do this to him?

Let us turn back the pages of time to a few months before this tragic event occurred and see.

3   John 1:11
4   Galatians 4:4
5   1 Corinthians 10:4

Crucified

Chapter Two
The Feast of Dedication

> *"Then came the Feast of Dedication at Jerusalem. It was winter, and Jesus was in the temple area walking in Solomon's Colonnade."*
> John 10:22-23

The main entrance into the temple, known as the Beautiful Gate, opened up into the Women's court, and as one entered the area he was welcomed by a breathtaking view of the sanctuary with its gold overlaid columns, rising 150 feet, standing tall above the outer court. Herod was a great builder, and had done an extraordinary job during his reign in making the temple one of the most awe-inspiring structures of its day[1]. He did so more out of a desire to impress Rome than honor God. But impressive it was none-the-less. Outside of the temple proper, along the eastern side of the outer court was the Great Porch, or Colonnade named after

1 Unger, page 114,115

Solomon. It was a large covered area with an upper balcony supported by 162 beautiful columns rising 100 feet tall.

The Feast of Dedication, sometimes known as the Feast of Lights, was a special observance celebrating the rededication of the Temple under Judas Maccabaeus in 164 BC.[2] It took place in the first few weeks of December. For eight nights the great temple was lit up with an abundance of candles and lamps to show off its splendor.[3] The people gathered and chanted Psalm 113 and Psalm 118, known as *the Hallel*[4]. They gathered each evening amidst the tall columns of the temple, its gold glittering by candlelight, their voices rose in unison:

"Praise the LORD!
Praise, O servants of the LORD,
Praise the name of the LORD.
Blessed be the name of the LORD from this time forth and forever.
From the rising of the sun to its setting
The name of the LORD was to be praised."

They did not realize it, but the Lord they were praising was about to enter the temple.

Jesus came to this feast to celebrate the temple of God. He was a Galilean, and most of his ministry over the past three years took place in that region. Because he was a Jew, Jerusalem held a special place in his heart.

---

[2] 1 Macc.vi. 52-59
[3] This was the forerunner and roots of the Jewish holiday we know today as "Hanukkah," which is the Hebrew word for "Dedication."
[4] Edersheim, The Temple – Its Ministry and Services, Ch 14, pg 429

He came here each year to celebrate the Passover and other great feast days. Even as a young boy he loved this place, once slipping away from his parents so he could spend time in the beautiful house of his Father.⁵

Now, as a well-known teacher and healer, he entered the temple area and began to stroll down Solomon's Porch. Soon the crowds recognized him and gathered around until his walk was brought to an abrupt end. There was a chill in the December air. It was winter-time in Jerusalem, but the chill Jesus felt as he stood before the majestic columns of Solomon's court came not from the winter air, but from certain members of the crowd that followed him. Certain men waited and watched for him.⁶

One of these antagonists stepped forward and asked sarcastically, "How long will you keep us in suspense? If you are the Christ, tell us plainly." Jesus' dark eyes quickly focused upon the man, calmly yet firmly he replied, "I told you, and you do not believe." The crowd stilled as Jesus continued, "The works I do in my Father's name, these testify of me. But you do not believe because you are not of my sheep." Then looking to the attentive faces in the audience he continued, "My sheep hear my voice, and I know them and they follow me. My Father, who has given them to me, is greater than all; and no one is able to snatch them out of the Father's hand." Then glancing heavenward, he proclaimed to the growing crowd, "I and the Father are one." ⁷

The antagonists in the audience jumped on this last statement. One with God? "Blasphemy!" they shouted. As in his previous visit a few

---

5   Luke 2:45-49
6   John 11:57
7   John 10:24-31

months before, the crowd was divided[8]. Some reached down and found stones that were lying about. Others quickly gathered up a few rocks which were propping up candle stands and lamps. They rushed to the front of the crowd ready to stone this blasphemer.

Jesus stopped them in their tracks as he raised his voice, "I showed you many good works from the Father; for which of them are you stoning me?" With stones in hand they moved closer, "Because you being a man make yourself out to be God!" they replied as they moved in to take him. Jesus stepped aside, and in the flickering shadows of the crowd and the confusion of the moment he slipped away, out one of the many side gates and into the countryside.[9]

Jerusalem had become a dangerous place for the Lord. This was not the first time they had tried to stone him in the temple.[10] The Pharisees had poisoned the atmosphere and the High Priest had lit a fuse of hatred that would burn all the way to Calvary.

Jesus' next visit to the City of David would be his last. His enemies would be better prepared next time.

---

8   John 10:19-21
9   John 10:39
10   John 8:59

Chapter Three

Bethany Beyond the Jordan

> *"And he went away again beyond the Jordan to the place where John was first baptizing, and he was staying there."*
>
> John 10:40

The Jordan River begins in the hill country of Galilee and Lebanon, winds its way down the length of the Promise Land, and empties into the Dead Sea. The famous river is fed by wadis that flood its banks and muddy its water. Thick growths of reeds and thickets along its shores gave refuge to wild beasts and thieves. The prophet Jeremiah had spoken of lions that would come up "from the thickets of the Jordan."[1] Throughout its history it did not have the best of reputations.[2]

1 Jeremiah 49:19
2 2 Kings 5:12

To the southern region of its banks came John the Baptist, to Bethany beyond the Jordan.[3] It was three or four miles east of Jericho, in the wilderness on the eastern banks of the river[4] not far from where it empties into the Dead Sea. Here John found deep pools along the river's edge suitable for baptizing[5] and where he both began and completed his life's work.

Now a small band of travelers had come to this place of isolation and safety. Jesus and his beloved Twelve, and some of his more dedicated disciples, had ended their celebration of the temple early. They slipped away from Jerusalem and walked seventeen miles east down the steep road to Jericho, where they had tried to pass unnoticed. From there it was just a few more miles to the Jordan River. It was more than a day's walk from Jerusalem. As they came upon the Jordan, they began to search for a good place to cross.

Some of the Apostles were very familiar with this area. This was where a few of them had first met Jesus, among whom was Andrew. As he walked along Jordon's shore Andrew thought back to that day he first saw the man who would change his life. Word had spread of a great prophet named John who was preaching and baptizing in the Jordan. Andrew and his brother, along with a young fisherman friend named John,

---

3   John 1:28
4   The location of Bethany beyond the Jordan, the scene of John's baptizing, has not been positively identified. Some believe it had a northern location, a few miles south of the Sea of Galilee, while others believe it to have a southern location, just east of Jericho,. The Scriptures support the latter. Matthew 3:5-6 tells us concerning John's ministry, "Jerusalem was going out to him, and all Judea and all the district around the Jordan" to be baptized of him. This would indicate a southern location, near Jericho. We also read in Matthew 3:13 that Jesus had to leave Galilee to come find John to be baptized by him. Thus, the scriptures seem to give greater support to the southern area of the Jordan, as being this "Bethany beyond the Jordan." Archeologists believe it was in the vicinity of the wilderness around the Wadi El-Kharrar and near the Hajlah Ford.
5   John 3:23

had come from Galilee to find this prophet and listen to his message of repentance. This wilderness prophet stayed away from the cities. He was unsociable and unorthodox. He dressed in a strange garment made of camel hair, with a leather belt about it. His diet consisted mostly of grasshoppers, wild honey, and such.[6] The Pharisees and Sadducees would come to hear him, but dismissed him as a crazy man. "He has a demon," they would say.[7]

Andrew recalled standing near John the baptizer, and saw him point to a man walking toward him and proclaim, "Behold the Lamb of God." Andrew and his friend began to follow this man around until he turned and asked what they wanted. They would spend the rest of the day with this man, called Jesus. Andrew could still recall searching through the large crowd later that day until he found his brother Simon Peter and introduced him to his new teacher.[8] Now they had returned to this familiar place of pleasant memories.

There were memories here for Jesus as well. John baptized him in this area of the Jordan. With a smile Jesus recalled his cousin's reluctance to do so. "No, no!" John exclaimed, "I am not even worthy of unlatching your sandals!" he said.[9] That day seemed distant now. Things had changed so much since that happy day, the day his proud heavenly Father had spoken from above.

The cold winter water felt good to their weary feet as they crossed the river. With some bread from the city, a few fish from the river, and a

---

6   Matthew 3:4
7   Matthew 11:18
8   John 1:35-42
9   John 1:27

warm fire to dry clothes and cook a meal, the tired group of men settled in for some rest. As evening came Jesus lay near the warmth of the fire and gazed up into the starry face of his Father. He thought back to that scene in the temple and knew that things would get worse. For now they had some solitude. For now they had escaped the danger. For now there was restful sleep under the music of Jordan's flowing waters.

Chapter Four

"Lazarus Is Sick"

> *"Many came to Him and were saying, 'While John performed no sign, yet everything John said about this man was true.' Many believed in Him there."*
>
> John 10:41-42

The solitude along the Jordan did not last long. Many in the crowd that day in the temple wanted to hear more from the prophet from Galilee and were eager to find this great teacher. The search began: one saw some of his disciples gathering bread in the market the next day; then a traveler from Jericho saw a group walking east. In Jericho, there was word was that the prophet had settled in beyond the Jordan. It took only a few days for them to find their man.

They knew of Jesus' miracles and were familiar with John's teachings about Jesus. As they walked toward the Jordan to the place where the Baptist had taught, they discussed his teachings and realized what John said about Jesus was true.[1]

Within days many feet crossed over the Jordan's chilly waters seeking the teacher from Galilee. Jesus responded with compassion, and for hours he sat and taught them. For hours they listened, bundled up in the winter air, and were spellbound by his words. Like the temple officers had said, "Never has a man spoken the way this man speaks."[2] As they listened, many were convinced that this Jesus was the "Christ," the awaited savior of Israel.

During these weeks, Jesus and his entourage stayed on the move. There were cities and villages in the vicinity that Jesus wanted to visit.[3] It did not take long before this great celebrity of Israel once again began to attract large crowds.[4] On one occasion someone in the crowd asked, "Lord, is there just a few who will be saved?" He said to them, "Strive to enter through the narrow door; for many, I tell you, will seek to enter and will not be able."[5]

With his location established, the Pharisees in the area followed him about, keeping an eye on him, and testing him at every opportunity.[6] In

---

1 John 10:41
2 John 7:46
3 Luke 13:22; When Jesus heard the news about Lazarus he said "let us go to Judea again." So Jesus was not at that time in the region of Judea, indicating that this trip recorded by Luke kept him on the other side of the Jordan. Herod had a palace to the south of where Jesus was encamped, probably where John the Baptist was arrested and beheaded. It seems Jesus may have been in this area when he received the news of Lazarus' illness.
4 Luke 14:25
5 Luke 13:23-24
6 Luke 11:53-54

"Lazarus Is Sick"

one village a Pharisee invited Jesus into his home on the Sabbath to have bread with him. There was a man present who suffered from dropsy. Noticing the man, Jesus turned and asked his host, "Is it lawful to heal on the Sabbath?" The Pharisee, and a few lawyers who were present, looked at one another in silence. Jesus then walked over, took hold of the man, and healed him. As the man left the room overjoyed, Jesus turned to those present and asked, "Which of you will have a son or an ox fall into a well, and will not immediately pull him out on a Sabbath day?" Again they were silent, but their silence spoke of their contempt.[7]

As Jesus was teaching in one of these villages some messengers came to him with news. This news would greatly impact the remaining days of Jesus upon the earth. The message had been sent by Mary and Martha, back in Bethany. The news was not good; "Lord, your friend Lazarus whom you love is sick." Jesus' initial response was encouraging. "This sickness is not to end in death, but for the glory of God, so that the Son of God may be glorified by it." One would think that the Great Physician would hasten to be at the bedside of his friend. But he did not, for Jesus knew that in the day it had taken for these men to arrive with their plea that Lazarus had already died. He would let his friend sleep a while longer.[8] There were still large crowds to be taught and a greater miracle was waiting. Jesus went about his business for two more days.[9]

These days were filled with rich teaching. The Pharisees and the scribes murmured against Jesus for associating with sinners. In his defense Jesus told three of his greatest parables - the lost sheep, the lost

7 Luke 14:1-6
8 John 11:13
9 John 11:6

coin, and the prodigal son.[10] At the end of the two days Jesus gathered up his Twelve in the fading hours of daylight. He announced to them that he needed to go and be with Lazarus and his family. "Let's go back to Judea," he said.[11] There was a quick response from his men. The rumble that spread from Peter to John and from Thomas to Bartholomew expressed doubt and alarm at their Lord's decision. "But Rabbi," they said, "a short while ago the Jews tried to stone you, and yet you are going back there?"[12] Jesus understood the dangers they expressed, but was not about to let fears for his own life affect his decision.

"Are there not twelve hours of daylight?" Jesus argued. "A man who walks by day will not stumble, for he sees by this world's light. It is when he walks by night that he stumbles for he has no light."[13] Jesus had never hidden in the darkness. He would live his life in the daylight, and he would finish his work in the twelve hours given to him. His men's argument, while appreciated, did not carry the day.

To seal the decision, Jesus broke the news about Lazarus to them which he had known all along. "Our friend Lazarus has fallen asleep; but I am going there to wake him up." For a moment their spirits were lifted; they knew that sleep was a good sign of a recovery.[14] "Perhaps he is getting better," they thought. But Jesus dashed their hopes when he spoke plainly to them, "No, Lazarus is dead. But I am glad I was not there, so

---

10   The material in Luke 15 and 16 is difficult to place in the chronology of the other writers, particularly John's Gospel. It contains rich teachings and therein is the emphasis with little information to identify it in the events of the day. See Robertson's note #10, p 276.
11   John 11:7
12   John 11:8
13   John 11:9-10
14   John 11:12

that you will be able to see something that will make you believe. Let us go to his tomb." [15]

His men sat for a moment in silence. They had been with Jesus for three years and now were concerned for his life. They knew of the danger, a danger that awaited them all if they headed toward Jerusalem again. Their faith, still lacking, was unable to understand what good Jesus could do for someone who was now dead and buried some distance away. But they had come this far with him. They glanced at one another. There was no discussion necessary; they were not about to desert their leader now. Thomas stood, threw his cloak about his shoulders in the growing coolness of the evening, and expressed the feelings of the group, "Let us also go that we may die with him."[16]

Thomas may have been a pessimist, but he was no coward.

---

15   John 11:15
16   John 11:16

Chapter Five

Return to Bethany

> *"So when Jesus came, He found that he had already been in the tomb four days. Now Bethany was near Jerusalem, about two miles off."*
>
> John 11:17-18

Quickly they walked through the morning darkness, their sandals striking up a rhythmical cadence upon the rocky road. A few dedicated disciples followed this band of brothers, thirteen strong. Walking close to the Lord was Peter, his hand occasionally coming to rest upon the short Roman style sword tucked into his waistband.[1] With the alert eyes of a fisherman, he looked into the horizon for any sign of danger as the sun began to lighten the sky.

1   John 18:10

As the warm noonday sun began to sink low in the winter sky, they drew near to Bethany. Jesus stopped to rest as one of the disciples went on ahead to announce to Lazarus' family the imminent arrival of the Master. Usually the Lord's arrival at Lazarus' home was a time of excitement and joy. That was not the case today. His dear friend had died. A deep sadness filled the Lord's heart. Before the sun set many tears would be shed. Some of the tears hitting Bethany's soil would be his own.

In this small town, a large crowd of family and friends were still gathered around the house of Lazarus. The funeral had taken place four days earlier, but the evident wealth and position of the family continued to attract a large gathering. They were there to mourn the loss of an influential citizen and comfort his survivors - sisters Mary and Martha.

As the word arrived to Martha that Jesus was drawing near, she slipped away from the crowd unnoticed and hurried to meet her brother's friend in a more private setting outside of town. She did not understand the delay of his coming, and in tones gently reproachful she lamented, "Lord, if you had been here my brother would not have died." Jesus answered with words that have brought comfort to the world ever since, "Your brother will rise again."[2]

Martha agreed that her brother would rise in the last great resurrection. Jesus replied, "I am the resurrection and the life; he who believes in me will live even if he dies; and everyone who lives and believes in me will never die. Do you believe this?" While Martha had seemed at times to be distracted from Jesus' teachings by her attention to cooking and caring for the Lord, her reply would indicate otherwise. She answered,

[2] John 11:20-26

"Yes, Lord; I have believed that you were the Christ, the son of God, even he who comes into the world."[3]

Martha returned to the house while Jesus waited on the road outside of town. She led Mary away to a private room and told her the news, "The Master is here," she said, "and is asking for you." Mary, thrilled by the news, rushed out of the house to find the Lord. The mourners saw her rush out and believed that in her grief she was returning to the tomb. They followed.[4]

When Mary saw the figure of Jesus ahead, her pace quickened. Soon she was rushing toward the Lord and fell at his feet. Amidst her own sobs she repeated that which she and her sister had been lamenting for days, "Lord, if you had been here my brother would not have died." As the crowd of mourners arrived and began to gather around, the air became filled with cries of grief and the ground covered with falling tears. In a tender voice Jesus asked, "Where have you laid him?" Mary stood and wiped her tears away, "Come and see, Lord." The hurt and pain which death had brought to such dear souls, the thought of the cruel suffering Lazarus had to experience, overwhelmed the Son of Man.

Jesus wept.

Mary led him through the crowd toward the tomb. The young Apostle, John, was taking all of this in. He had never seen the Lord so overwhelmed by emotion. He heard some proclaim, "See how he loved him!" Others wondered out loud why he had not come sooner and healed him. "He opened the eyes of the blind," was overheard, as they all turned and followed the trail of tears.

[3] John 11:23-27
[4] John 11:28-31

Chapter Six
"Lazarus, Come Forth"

"So Jesus, again being deeply moved within, came to the tomb. Now it was a cave, and a stone was lying against it."
John 11:38

This experience was one of the most gut-wrenching, emotional events in the Lord's earthly life. Outside of his Apostles, Lazarus was his closest friend. Martha had cared for him like a mother, and Mary had been one of his most dedicated students.[1] Now all their lives had been shaken by the death of this wonderful brother and friend.

As a man of some wealth, Lazarus had been buried in a cave, a hewn out tomb, wherein there would be several "beds" carved into the stone

---
1   Luke 10:38-42

walls. Some of these tombs might have provided spaces for four bodies, others as many as ten or fifteen. A rock would be rolled over the tomb to protect it from thieves and animals. Often a garden would surround the tomb. Now to this place of repose and death came the "Resurrection and the Life."

The crowd gathered around the site. It was an impressive gathering, Jesus and his twelve Apostles, dedicated disciples who were also traveling with them, Mary and Martha, and many friends, some of them influential and well-known people in Judea.

It was an emotional scene as well. For Jesus his spirit was deeply stirred.[2] The anguish of such a large number of people created an atmosphere of great sadness. The scene of the tomb with its large stone emphasized death's impenetrable barrier. The Apostles stood silent, as their own faith wavered. They knew of his power, but a body, dead four days might have been too much even for their Lord. The crowd was filled with believers and doubters alike when it came to Jesus' claims. Now they all came to this tomb, to this moment in time, to this place of death, and wondered what the prophet from Nazareth would or could do. As they gathered around the tomb, the sobs of the crowd drifted amid the air while the sun began to settle below the distant hillside. A lone figure stepped forward and the crowd grew silent.

"Roll back the stone," Jesus said. There was an immediate gasp in the audience, and even his own Apostles looked at him in amazement. Could Jesus want to gaze upon the face of Lazarus now? A face so contorted by death! Martha was totally taken aback by the statement and rushed

[2] John 11:38

forward to stand between the Lord and the stone. "Lord by this time there will be a stench," she humbly protested, "for he has been dead four days now." Jesus' answer was both tender and comforting as he gazed down into her tearful eyes, "Did I not say to you that if you believe, you will see the glory of God?"

With his words Martha's apprehension gave way to trust, and humbly she gave her approval to remove the stone. The crowd stood frozen in the moment, as some of Jesus' own stepped forward. The zealous Peter, the youthful John, the pessimistic Thomas, the eager Andrew, even the old tax collector Matthew - they all stepped forward and threw their weight and collective strength against the large stone. The grunting of men exerting great effort blended with the sound of stone upon stone as the rock was rolled back. Their task done the men stepped back in fearful respect of the grave and the dead. Before the open darkness of the tomb, Jesus stood alone, and lifting his eyes to the heavens, he prayed:

"Father I thank You that You have heard me. I knew that You always hear me; but because of the people standing around I said it, so that they may believe that You sent me."

Ending his prayer, he turned his gaze into the darkness of the tomb. In a voice heard all the way into Abraham's bosom, he cried out, "Lazarus, come forth!"

The eyes of Martha quickly turned from the Lord to the tomb. Mary rushed up to her side. They stood arm and arm, and in that moment they believed, they believed that with the Lord, it was possible!

The crowd stood spellbound. The Apostles, in fearsome apprehension, stepped back further from the rock, as their heartbeats quickened. In the ensuing silence a shuffling sound began to come from the deep recesses of the tomb. The sound grew stronger and then a vague image began to appear. Cries of disbelief spread through the crowd as men stepped back in fear and women collapsed in shock.

Then at last there he stood! A figure in white, bound head to toe in the winding cloths of his burial. Even his face remained covered in the traditional wrapping of the napkin. With a glint of joy in his eyes, Jesus turned to the sisters, who were standing stunned in the moment, "Unbind him and let him go."[3]

They rushed to their brother.

---

[3] John 11:44

Chapter Seven
The Plot to Kill

> *"Therefore many of the Jews who came to Mary, and saw what he had done, believed in him. But some of them went to the Pharisees and told them the things which Jesus had done."*
>
> John 11:45-46

In many ways the raising of Lazarus was Jesus' greatest miracle. Yes, he had raised the dead before. There was that young man, the widow's son, but that had happened in the obscure village of Nain in Galilee. [1] This time Jesus brought back from the dead a well-known and respected man just two miles from Jerusalem's city gates. He did so before a large crowd of influential and well-known Judeans,[2] and in the dramatic fash-

---
1   Luke 7:11-17
2   John 12:17-18; those who witnessed Lazarus' resurrection became a powerful force in convincing others to follow Jesus. To be so influential, some of them were surely well-known and respected citizens.

ion of a man dead four days. Many of the eyewitnesses were convinced; Jesus was the Messiah!

The news of this miracle reached Jerusalem like a wild fire coming over Olive's brow, spreading from tongue to tongue, from house to house, from shop to shop. It captured the attention of believers and skeptics alike. It was devastating news to Caiaphas the high priest and his group of Pharisees who had opposed this man's claims and ignored his power from the beginning.

Caiaphas was beside himself. He sent out word of a meeting. All the leaders were summoned to an emergency gathering of the Sanhedrin, the official court of Israel. Into the temple, up the stairs to the second floor of Solomon's porch, into the grand meeting hall of the religious and civic courts they went. As the meeting was called to order, it was evident that the raising of Lazarus had caused such a stir that the men feared its repercussions might reach all the way to Rome.[3]

"This man keeps on doing great signs. If we let him go on, pretty soon everyone will believe in him, and the Romans will come and remove what little power and privilege we have left."[4] If he was the Messiah, they feared, he would take over power and establish a new kingdom. This would surely offend Rome, and they would come and destroy them all.

It was one big mess, but they had no one to blame but themselves. They had opposed Jesus from the beginning. Their haughtiness and hypocrisy had twisted their views of this good man from day one. They never considered even once that he could be the promised Messiah, and

---

3   John 11:48
4   John 11:48

never took an honest look at his background or credentials. Their judgmental attitude blinded them from the beginning. Had they listened carefully, they would have known that Jesus had never spoken out against Rome. Even Pilate would not be concerned when he interviewed Jesus and learned that this man had no interest in any rebellion against Rome and his followers would not be encouraged to resist Roman rule.[5]

From that first day some of the Pharisees traveled to Galilee and saw this carpenter from Nazareth and his disciples plucking the grain and eating it on the Sabbath, they had been against him.[6] Within the week they began to conspire how they might destroy him.[7] Within a week! Soon their accusations began to fly:

"He does his signs by the power of Beelzebub!"[8]

"He breaks the Sabbath!"[9]

"He blasphemes by claiming to have the power to forgive sins!" [10]

And the action that really stuck in their craw; "He eats with tax collectors and sinners!"[11]

But none of the charges ever affected his popularity, and now all Jerusalem was abuzz with his latest great sign. Pacing the floor of their upper chamber their voices cried out in frustration. "How much longer can we tolerate this," said one. "It is time to take matters into our own hands," said another. In the midst of this heated debate, Caiaphas stepped forward and said; "You know nothing at all! You do not realize that it is

5 John 18:36
6 Matthew 12:1-2
7 Matthew 12:14
8 Matthew 12:24; Mark 3:22
9 Mark 3:2
10 Luke 5:21
11 Luke 5:30

The Plot to Kill

better for you that one man die for the people than that the whole nation perish."[12] Without realizing it, he had proclaimed Jesus as the true paschal lamb whose blood would atone for the sins of the world. However, his audience was not in the spirit to comprehend such a grand concept. Instead they only heard that this man must die "to save our nation!"[13]

Eating With Sinners

At that point the meeting turned into an assassination plot; When? How? Where? They had little power outside the city, so they must lie in wait for his return. But when he did re-enter the city, they must be ready to act. They must be ready to kill.

12   John 11:49-52
13   John 11:53

Road To The Upper Room

As these men walked out of their meeting hall, a few, a precious few, were keeping a deeply-kept secret; they believed that this Jesus was at least a great prophet and perhaps the Messiah himself.[14] Two of these men, Joseph of Arimathea and Nicodemus,[15] were deeply troubled with the decision that had just been made.

They must warn the Lord. He must not try to enter Jerusalem again.

14 John 12:42
15 John 19:38-39

Chapter Eight
Ephraim and Galilee

> *"Therefore Jesus no longer continued to walk publicly among the Jews, but went away from there to the country near the wilderness, into a city called Ephraim; and there he stayed with the disciples."*
>
> John 11:54

What a joy it was for Jesus to observe the Sabbath in the home of Lazarus. Their friendship now had a unique bond. In the quietness of Lazarus' home, he and Jesus would sit off in a corner and whisper about things concerning death and the hereafter that no one else could ever know. Martha kept the two friends well nourished, while Mary tried as often as possible to listen in on their conversations.

Lazarus himself had quickly reached celebrity status. Every day

Road To The Upper Room

strangers came by to see the man who had lain in the tomb for four days.[1] Among the visitors was someone sent, perhaps by Nicodemus,[2] with word of the secret meeting and the decision of the Sanhedrin - the High Priest had put out an arrest warrant for Jesus. They wanted him dead. However, confronting these forces in Jerusalem at this time was not in the plans. Jesus was destined to wait until the Passover came. But the messenger's information confirmed that he could not stay in Bethany either. For now he would buy some time by heading north into less populated land. There he could stay out of sight for the weeks before the Passover. As the sun rose on another winter day, Jesus and his Apostles left Bethany and headed north. They went into Samaria toward Galilee.

The road north from Bethany took them by Jerusalem in the early morning hours. As they descended the hillside of the Mount of Olives, they stopped for a few moments at one of the Lord's favorite resting places. It was a small orchard of olive trees, called Gethsemane, with a press to harvest the oil. Here Jesus paused to gaze upon the great City of David.

Through the limbs of the large olive trees, Jesus' eyes were drawn across the Kidron valley to a beautiful view of the city and Mount Zion. It was on Zion's peak that the majestic temple stood. The city and the temple were surrounded by a great wall, originally built under the reconstruction efforts of Nehemiah over four hundred years before, and improved upon by Herod. Jesus had a clear view of the point where the temple wall and the city wall came together over the valley below, a place known as the "pinnacle of the temple." He could remember the day Satan brought

---

[1] See John 12:9
[2] Edersheim, The Life and Times of Jesus the Messiah, vol. 2 Sec. 21, Pg 477

In Ephraim, Jesus Enjoys Some Solitude

him to that spot and invited him to cast himself down and let the angels catch him in their arms. He resisted Satan's temptations on that occasion, but sadly knew as he gazed beyond Gethsemane's trees that much of the city's leadership was under Lucifer's strong influence.

These final few months of Jesus' life were emotional ones. As he passed by a city he had loved since the days of David, he longed to reach out to his beloved Israel.

Down from the heights of Zion they walked. With gravity as their friend, the group moved quickly from the rocky mountain trails into the fertile valleys that "flowed with milk and honey." Jesus moved into Samaria and settled into the little village of Ephraim.[3] He stayed there with some of his disciples. He did not wish to return all the way into Galilee; there were too many people, too many spies. For a few weeks at least Ephraim would become home. It was a small village, but Jesus had good friends there who provided lodging and food for their numbers. This village was off the beaten path and offered some seclusion away from the malignity of his enemies, which had grown more intense. It made for a perfect little retreat. During this time they repaired old sandals, mended coats, and sent messengers to their wives and families in Galilee.

It was the last time Jesus would enjoy some real solitude. His mood was clearly changing, and at times his heartbeat quickened as he realized that the reality of the cross was only a few short weeks away. The weather began to warm as springtime slowly dawned upon the land. They all

---

3   John 11:54 The city of Ephraim has not been exactly located. But most research puts it near Bethel. Perhaps the Hebrew spelling was Ephron. It was a few miles off the main road between Galilee and Jerusalem, and therefore was a secluded village in the area leading down the rocky gorges toward the Jordan River.

Ephraim and Galilee

knew that the Passover feast would not be far away. His Apostles were enjoying the warmer days, but it was hard to ignore the change in their Master's mood. "Do you think he will return to Jerusalem for the feast?" they quietly debated among themselves. They knew of the dangers there, yet they reminded each other of how he had ignored the danger before. It was beyond their grasp that he had escaped the previous attempts upon his life because it was not his hour. Nor could they understand now that his hour was near, only that his mood was changing.

One morning Jesus let it be known to the Twelve that they would be going to Jerusalem for the Passover.[4] Immediate preparations were begun. The celebration of the Passover was the biggest event of the year and was celebrated by entire families. Bidding goodbye to the safety of Ephraim, Jesus and the Apostles traveled up to the border of Samaria and Galilee, gathering up their families along the way.[5] Most of the Apostles, as well as Jesus' brothers, were married men.[6] Soon the group became quite large in number, as many women and children joined them.[7] Along the way Mary, the mother of Jesus, was reunited with her son, along with her sister. Also meeting up with them was Mary from Magdala, a small town near Capernaum. She was the forever grateful disciple healed by the Lord. Among the growing caravan were some of the mothers of the Apostles, such as Mary the mother of James, and also Mary the mother of the "sons of Zebedee" (James and John).[8]

4   Luke 18:31
5   Luke 17:11, Matthew 19:1, Mark 10:1
6   1 Corinthians 9:5
7   Mark 15:41
8   The text was clear as to the many women who were present on this trip and in Jerusalem during this final week. It was an impressive group. Many women traveled with Jesus and his disciples as did their children as well. See Matthew 27:55, John 19:25, and Matthew 20:20. Some of these women would also be the first to witness Jesus' resurrection.

Road To The Upper Room

During this time, as they were entering a certain village, a small group of men stood some distance away, and cried out to Jesus, "Master, have pity on us!" These were nine Jews and one Samaritan who suffered the deadly, awful disease of leprosy. Forbidden from the cities, this small band of contagious men roamed the wilderness areas of Samaria. With only a slow awful death awaiting them, they cried out in desperation to a man they had heard was a great healer. Jesus answered their cries for help, "Go, show yourselves to the priests," he instructed them. As they went in an act of obedient faith, new blood began to flow through their veins, and rotting flesh became pure before their very eyes. The nine Jews hurried away to find a priest, while the lone Samaritan looked back to the Master. No longer bound by the law to keep his distance, he came running and shouting for joy to the heavens and fell at Jesus' feet. His words were simple and sincere, "Thank you!"

Jesus looked over the crowds that surrounded him, and asked, "Where are the nine?" Then turning to the crowd, "Look, only one has returned to praise God, and he is a Samaritan!" He sent the grateful man on his way, "Your faith has made you whole." [9] Once again Jesus praised the often-despised Samaritans.

With his caravan complete, Jesus turned his face toward Jerusalem, and like Moses leading his people to Sinai, he led his family and disciples toward Zion.

---

9   Luke 17:11-19

Chapter Nine

Return to Jerusalem

> *"While He was on His way to Jerusalem, He was passing between Samaria and Galilee."*
>
> Luke 17:11

One route from Galilee to Jerusalem traveled on the east side of the Jordan River, sometimes referred to as the "region of Judea beyond the Jordan."[1] It was this path Jesus and his group traveled, going around Samaria and crossing back over near Jericho. With the Passover drawing near and springtime coming into full bloom, the roadway began to fill with caravans of happy pilgrims.[2] The elderly men and women accompanying

1   Matthew 19:1; Mark 10:1
2   John 11:55

Road To The Upper Room

them insured that the pace would be slow, giving playful children time to run about. Donkeys were pulled along with heavy supplies tied to their backs, while small herds of sheep followed the voice of their shepherds toward the altars of Jerusalem.

The group was slowed by the popularity of Jesus. Back out in the public eye, the multitudes came again, and as always, he taught them and healed their sick. The Pharisees were around as well, still asking difficult questions in vain attempts to trap him in some legal blunder.[3]

On one occasion as Jesus was teaching, some of the women brought their babies wanting Jesus to touch them.[4] Many children also came with them and wanted to see him. But the disciples held them back. When the Lord saw what was happening he was angry, "Let the children come," he ordered! Set free, the children ran to him, getting as close to this special man as they could. He patted the babies on their heads, took some of the children up into his arms and blessed them saying, "Of such is the kingdom of heaven."[5]

Along the way, as the Lord's caravan traveled Jordan's path, a young man drew near. Unable to contain his excitement, he ran toward Jesus and knelt at his feet. "Teacher, what good thing must I do to get eternal life?" he inquired. Jesus immediately took a liking to this young man, yet his answer was to the point. "Obey the commandments... sell what you have... and follow me." The young man walked away in sorrow, for he loved his money more than eternal life.[6] Had he followed the Lord on this

---

3   Matthew 19:3; Jesus answers questions about divorce.
4   Luke 18:15
5   Mark 10:13-16; Luke 18:15-17
6   Mark 10:17-22

journey – Oh! The things he would have seen!

Watching the man depart, Peter approached the Lord, remembering the day he and his brother had walked away from their nets, their boats, and a great catch of fish to become "fishers of men." "We have left everything to follow you!" his brawny voice said softly. "What then will there be for us?" Jesus was touched by his inquiry. Looking into the faces of his beloved men he answered, "When the Son of Man sits on his glorious throne; those who have followed me will also sit on twelve thrones, judging the twelve tribes of Israel." Then looking into the strong face of Peter, he assured him that for their dedication, even to the point of forsaking their own families, they would "receive a hundred times as much and will inherit eternal life."

As Jerusalem drew nearer and the weather warmer, he became more solemn and isolated. He walked ahead of the group, a lone figure against the growing mountain horizon. His disciples gazed upon him and reminded each other of the dangers that waited in Jerusalem. Fear overwhelmed them - fear for their Master, their son, their brother, their friend. How could he return to this place knowing the dangers? They were astonished at his courage and resolve.[7]

At day's end he assembled his twelve Apostles together. These twelve men had done what the young man a few days before would not do. They had taken every step with Jesus for the past three years. He needed to tell them that their time together was about to come to an end. He had to be honest with them, as he always had, and somehow find the words to speak plainly of what was about to happen in Jerusalem. This time he

7   Mark 10:32

would not escape the mob, nor flee to the north. This time his hour had come.

"We are going up to Jerusalem," he said. "And the Son of Man will be betrayed to the chief priests and teachers of the law. They will condemn him to death and will hand him over to the Gentiles, who will mock him and spit on him, flog him and kill him. Three days later he will rise." [8]

Their worst fears were confirmed.

On Jordan's banks they stood. A thousand years before Israel had crossed with joyous hearts as they marched over into the Promised Land. Now a smaller group of God's chosen people crossed over, wading the rain swollen banks. The children laughed and played as they crossed the muddy waters, while young mothers clutched their babies tightly. There was excitement in the air as the crossing signaled the nearness of Jericho and Jerusalem. Yet twelve men walked with a secret fear within their hearts and an evident sadness upon their faces as they were led forward by one solitary figure.

It was now seven days before the Passover.

---

[8] Mark 10:32-34

The Narrative

Section Two:
The Last Week

Chapter One
The City of Palms

"He entered Jericho, and was passing through."
Luke 19:1

From the top of Mount Pisgah, Moses gazed upon the valley of Jericho, the "city of palms."[1] After the great walls of Jericho came down under Joshua's invasion, a new city was built a half mile north of the ancient site. When Elisha took over the mantle of Elijah, he returned to the city of Jericho, where the men of the city came to him and immediately tested his powers. "Our city is well situated," they said, "but the waters of the springs are bad and cause the land to be unproductive, and some of our

[1] Deuteronomy 34:1-3

Road To The Upper Room

own have died from drinking this bad water." Elisha asked for a new jar of salt and cast it into the springs, and the water became pure.[2]

Since that day the springs of Elisha had continued to flow down the valley of Jericho turning it into an oasis of palm trees, sycamores, cyprus flowers, and balsam plants. Antony presented Cleopatra with the gift of sweet-smelling balsam plantations, which she in turn sold to Herod the Great.[3] Herod liked this city, and with his son, built a summer palace surrounded with stately palms, gardens of roses, and aromatic balsam plants. The sweet aroma which drifted about the city on the warm breezes of this oasis may have given the city its name; Jericho - "the perfumed."

Jericho was a "priestly" city as well, meaning that a large number of priests lived within its city gates. It was also a city of great commerce. Through the city flowed the caravan route from Arabia and Damascus. Traders from far and near came to this Eden of Judah to purchase or sell. This made it a chief collection station for taxes by Rome. A large number of tax collectors worked to collect taxes on the imports and exports between the Roman province and the dominions of Herod Antipas.

As the Thursday afternoon sun began to set upon this little paradise, Jesus and his group of followers arrived at the city gates. They entered the city and began to make their way through its main street. The people of Jericho were accustomed to caravans and large bands of visitors. With word of who had entered the city, they stopped what they were doing and gathered to welcome and see for themselves the famous prophet from Galilee. Growing crowds lined the road and every eye strained to

---

2   2 Kings 2:18-22
3   Edersheim; The Life and Times of Jesus the Messiah, Book 4, Chapter 24, Pg 488

get a glimpse of the great miracle worker - Jesus of Nazareth.[4]

Taking into account the backdrop of the event, the scene of Jesus walking through Jericho, was one of the most interesting in Scripture. The Son of Man walked through this lush oasis on a warm spring afternoon, on his way to the barren hilltop of Golgotha. Behind him followed his "crowd"[5] consisting of the Apostles and the women and children that were a part of their families, including Jesus' beloved mother, Mary. How she beamed with joy seeing the multitudes rush to behold her son.

Caravan leaders deserted the market place, all wishing to see the prophet they had heard about throughout their travels. Roman guards abandoned their posts to check out all the commotion, and to maintain order if needed. A large number of priests joined the growing crowds, trying to act unimpressed by the arrival of Jesus, yet secretly longing to see this miracle-worker as much as their neighbors did. Pharisees pressed their way to the front, looking for an opportunity to engage Jesus as he passed by. Women held up their babies in hopes that the Healer's eyes might for a moment gaze upon them. Fathers pushed their children through the crowd so that someday, when they were old, they could tell of seeing the Messiah. The music of the marketplace and the sweet smell of balsam mingled with the joy of the crowd to make that moment the greatest moment in the history of Jericho since the day the walls came tumbling down.

4   Luke 19:3
5   Luke 18:36

Sitting at his table that day, the chief tax collector of the city noted that his customers had rushed out to join the crowds. "The prophet is coming," they shouted. Gathering up his day's receipts he also rushed out. Like Moses gazing upon the burning bush, he decided that he too must "turn aside and see this great sight."[6]

---

[6] Exodus 3:3

Chapter Two
"Zaccheus, Come Down"

> *"And there was a man called by the name of Zaccheus; he was a chief tax collector and he was rich."*
> Luke 19:2

As a tax collector, and a "chief" one as well, Zaccheus was one of the most despised men in the city. He was a Jew who worked for Rome to collect the hated taxes which supported their oppression by Caesar. He was wealthy before his appointment by Rome, and now oversaw the collection of taxes by many men who worked under him. He knew of Jesus and had heard how he spoke well of publicans and sinners. He even heard that he had elevated a tax collector to the office of Apostle! This was a man he must see for himself.

When he arrived at the main street he was overwhelmed by the crowd that had assembled. His four-foot-something height could not see over the masses in front of him.[1] Quickly he girded up his robe and began to run down the street to get in front of the crowd and the procession. His small feet made quick strides as he hastened to find a suitable place. The crowd thinned up ahead, but still the chance to see over them was hopeless. Glancing up he made a quick decision; casting his dignity aside, he climbed up into a sycamore tree by the roadway. Not the most graceful position perhaps, but as he pulled himself up limb over limb he at last had a wonderful view above the crowd. Soon the Lord made his way toward him with hundreds of others, all longing for a moment of attention from the Master.

Jesus came closer and closer. Then to the wee little man's amazement, he stopped just beneath him and looked up.

Zaccheus' heart stopped as all eyes followed the Lord's and gazed upon him in the tree. Some laughter went through the crowd as they viewed the hated tax collector caught out on a limb.

"Zaccheus," Jesus said, "Hurry down." The crowd, curious as to Jesus' intentions, grew silent. "Today is my day to be a guest in your home,"[2] announced the Master. The crowd's silence quickly turned to murmurs as the little man scurried down. "He does not despise me," he thought to himself as he dropped to his feet and hurried up to properly welcome this famous prophet who knew his name. With formalities out of the way,

---

[1] Luke 19:3 Only Luke gives us this account of Zaccheus.
[2] Luke 19:5; The Message

"Zaccheus, Come Down."

Zacchaeus was anxious to show Jesus and his followers the way to his home. The crowd that welcomed Jesus as a hero, now quickly changed their tune. "Were there no priests in this city that would have made better hosts?" they murmured. Priests and Pharisees grumbled among themselves, "He has gone to be the guest of a man who is a sinner!"[3]

Leading his guests toward his home, Zaccheus heard the cries of "sinner!" in the distance. He came to an abrupt halt and faced Jesus. He wanted to set the record straight. "Lord, half of my profits I have always given back to help the poor of this city," he said. "And now if any of my workers overtax anyone, and it comes to my attention, I correct the matter immediately and repay that individual four times the amount he was defrauded." [4]

Jesus too wanted to set the record straight, announcing to the crowd, "Today, salvation has come to this house, because he, too, is a son of Abraham. For the Son of Man has come to seek and to save that which was lost." With humility as lowly as his height, Zaccheus lead the Lord to his home.

With most of the crowd now gone, they arrived at the front gate of the tax collector's home. Jesus used this moment to face his group, and knowing that in their hearts they hoped that he would soon re-established the

---

3   Luke 19:7
4   Luke 19:8 While there was some scholarly discussion about this statement, as to whether or not Zaccheus was speaking of his past actions, or of his new intentions, it appears that the former seems more logical, and is within the wording and meaning of the text. "This view has in its favor the present tense of the verbs - `I give, I restore.' Since the Lord Jesus himself made a momentous argument for the immortality of the soul to turn on the tense of a single verb (Matthew 22:32f), they must be rash indeed who set aside the present tense in this passage in favor of future tense" (Coffman's commentary on this passage). Zaccheus was an honest and good man who was hated not because of any corruption, but because of his position as an employee of Rome.

kingdom of David in Jerusalem, he spoke a unique parable unto them;[5] "A nobleman went to a distant country to receive a kingdom for himself, and then returned." He told of the nobleman's slaves who were left behind to care for his business until he returned and upon that return he rewarded his slaves and punished his enemies. The message was presented, the lesson was plain; the kingdom would not come until the nobleman went away. Now that nobleman stood before the door of a publican, in the valley of Jericho, and knew that his departure was near. The shadow of the cross was growing heavier upon the mind of Jesus. Sadly, many of his disciples listening to the parable, "heard, but did not hear."

It was a good meal that evening as Zaccheus rolled out the red carpet for his guests. Jesus reclined around the table and looked into the faces of his Twelve dining around him. There was Matthew, a tax collector himself; Peter, Andrew, James and John, the four fishermen of Galilee; Philip and Bartholomew, two good-hearted Galileans; Thomas, the courageous one; Thaddaeus, the quiet one; James the son of Alpheus and Simon, the two Zealots fighting against Roman rule; and Judas Iscariot, the treasurer of the group. The nobleman's kingdom would soon rest in their hands. "Will they be up to the task?" Jesus wondered. Time would tell.

The next day Jesus would begin his final journey. He would lead his Apostles, his family, and his followers, to Bethany and on to Jerusalem. But like the man in whose home they now slept, his disciples could not see over the crowd, beyond the events of the day. For if they could, they would have understood the parable of the nobleman and the reason for Jesus' troubled spirit.

5   Luke 19:11

Chapter Three
From Jericho to Bethany

> *"Jesus, therefore, six days before the Passover, came to Bethany where Lazarus was, whom Jesus had raised from the dead."*
>
> John 12:1

The road from Jericho to Jerusalem was a difficult one. The rocky uphill passage went from 600 feet below sea level to 2500 feet above sea level. It was a steep, dangerous, robber-haunted, seventeen mile ascent that took strong men a good six hours to travel. The deep canyons gave hiding places to robbers, a fact which Jesus alluded to when he told his parable of a man who fell among thieves along this road and was left for dead.[1] It was a parable based upon well-known reality.

[1] Luke 10:30ff

Jesus woke his disciples before sunrise Friday morning for an early start. With the large number of women and children in their group, the ascent to Mount Zion would take them much longer than six hours - more like eight. Jesus knew that they needed to get to Bethany before sundown, when the Sabbath would begin. Bidding his new friend Zaccheus farewell, the Lord turned his face toward Jerusalem and lead his group of pilgrims out of Jericho and up the mountain slope. He last traveled this road when his friend Lazarus had died. Now he looks forward to a happier arrival in Bethany.

Jesus was a man in his early thirties, his work as a carpenter and his many travels by foot, had left him strong of body. His muscular legs made quick work of the rocky slope and his well-developed lungs inhaled the warm air, now growing thinner with each step, all with the fitness of an athlete. Upon his back he carried his mother's load with ease. He was able-bodied and in the prime of his life. His strength made quick work of the uphill road. However, a week later his body would be tested to its limits by the Roman scourge, his strength examined under the weight of the cross, his tolerance for pain put on display for all to see.

As the group made its way up the long, barren gorge to Bethany, the city of Jerusalem had already filled up with pilgrims from far and near. Some had arrived a week early to undergo the purification process; some had come from distant countries to enjoy the crowds, the markets, and the beauty of the temple. Over the months since the raising of Lazarus, the Sanhedrin's decision to arrest Jesus had become public. Anticipating his arrival, announcements were made wherever people gathered;

The Road "Up To Jerusalem."

"If anyone sees Jesus of Nazareth you must report it to the proper officials, so that he might be arrested."[2] The hatred that the High Priest, the Pharisees, the Sadducees, and the elders of the people had for Jesus was, however, not held by the masses of visitors who had come into the city. Yet these announcements made clear to all the dangers Jesus faced if he dared enter Jerusalem. But this was Passover, one of the most sacred and holy days of the Jewish year. "Will he come to the feast?" became the question asked on every street corner, in every home, and from one mighty pillar to the next down Solomon's porch.[3] The "man on the street" knew Jesus to be a great prophet and could not imagine him not coming to such an important event. But they also knew the disdain the religious leaders had for him. Would he come in defiance of their arrest warrant? If he did, what would be the outcome? In every language the people asked one another, "What do you think?" Already Jesus was the talk of the town.

Two miles away, on the road from Jericho, Jesus and his band of followers began to enter Bethany. It had been a difficult day's walk, but the younger helped the older and the group made good time. Jesus and his inner circle arrived at Lazarus' home, while others in the group fanned out to stay with friends and family, or camp as many did, outside Jerusalem in the valley of the Kidron, and about the western slopes of the Mount of Olives.[4]

As some of Jesus' group began to mingle with the visitors around the area, word spread that Jesus had arrived in Bethany and that he was stay-

[2] John 11:57
[3] John 11:56
[4] Farrar, p 325

ing with Lazarus. Over the past few months, Lazarus had become a living witness of the Lord's power and teachings. Because of his testimony, many of the Jews had come to believe in Jesus. The chief priests had discussed the growing problem Lazarus presented and could reach only one conclusion: they must kill Jesus and his well-known friend. [5] Lazarus must be put back in the tomb.

It had been a couple of months since Jesus had called Lazarus out of Abraham's bosom. He had left his friend because of the danger which had arisen in Jerusalem. Now he had returned, not because the danger had faded, but because his hour had now come.

In Saturday's dawn, Herod's glorious temple sat quiet, its gold shining in the sun. There was little stirring in the homes, tents, and campsites around the hillsides and valleys of Jerusalem. It was the time of the Sabbath rest as prescribed under Moses' Law. The Sabbath before the Passover had special importance and was called by the Jews the "Great Sabbath."[6] In the peace and comfort of Lazarus' home Jesus observed this special day for his last time.

As the sun set, a new week began. For many reasons it would be the greatest week in the history of mankind, as well as the most significant week in the eternity of the Godhead.

---

5 John 12:9-11
6 Farrar, footnote on p 493

Chapter Four
Anointed for Burial

"Mary then took a pound of very costly perfume of pure nard, and anointed the feet of Jesus and wiped his feet with her hair; and the house was filled with the fragrance of the perfume."

John 12:3

At sundown, as the "Great Sabbath" came to an end, a special supper was held in honor of Jesus' arrival.[1] It was held in Bethany in the home of a man named Simon. He had been healed of his leprosy and now invited

---

1   Arriving at the proper chronology of this event is not an easy task and can never be known for certain. Matthew (26:6-13) and Mark (14:3-9) place it two days before the Passover tying it closely to the betrayal of Judas. But their accounts only say the supper happened "while" Jesus was in Bethany. John was more specific about the exact day: "six days before the Passover… they made him a supper" (John 12:1-2). "On the next day" (John 12:12). It is hard to ignore a text when an exact day was specified, and accept another where no such specificity occurs. A special supper at the end of the "Great Sabbath" was in keeping with the times.

Jesus into his home as his special guest.[2] Lazarus was invited also; he had become almost as big of a celebrity as the Lord himself. Outside the home the crowds gathered around, anxious to see not only Jesus, but the famous man he had raised from the dead.[3] What a unique occasion to have both men around the same table! Simon could not help but beam with pride over the wonderful occasion taking place in his home. What a tremendous moment!

Also there were Lazarus' two sisters, Mary and Martha. During the meal it was evident that little had changed in the habits of the two women. Martha was busy serving the meal, while Mary sat as close to the Master as she could and took in his every word. This was the man who taught as no one else taught, and who had months before wept with her over her brother's death. This time she listened intently to the sound of his voice, a voice that had called her brother out of the recesses of that dark tomb.

As she listened, her love and adoration for the Lord and for the brother she had been given back could no longer be restrained. Not distracted by the serving of the meal as was her sister, she was in the moment moved to show some outward sign of her adoration and gratitude to the Lord who had so richly blessed her life.

Quietly she rose. In her hands she held a small vase. Unnoticed, she moved closer to the Lord. Reaching over his head as he was reclined

---

[2] Mark 14:3 Simon was called a leper but he would have had to have been cured in some way in order to be back in social circles. A healing by Jesus would endear him to the Master, and bring about this special supper. There was some supposition that Simon was the father of Martha, or that he had already died and Martha had inherited his home. The wording leaves all the above ideas as possibilities.
[3] John 12:9

Mary Anointing The Feet Of Jesus

around the table, she squeezed the clay neck of the vase until it broke and the expensive perfume within began to flow down upon the head of Jesus.[4] As the men around the table watched in stunned silence, Mary moved the vase from the Lord's head down to his feet. Oblivious to her audience, she uncovered her head and began to wipe up the excess oil with her long dark hair.

The fragrance of this nard filled the room with its sweet smell, as a few men came to their feet and quickly surrounded the Lord and his anointer. Believing this to be improper on many levels, they began to scold Mary for her actions. Leading in this criticism was one of Jesus' own - Judas Iscariot.

Judas, "the man of Kerioth," was of the tribe of Judah[5], and the only one of Jesus' Apostles who was not a Galilean. He was the treasurer for the group. He tended to the donations which the group received in order to pay expenses as they traveled. Now he complained over the actions of Mary.

"Why was this perfume not sold for three hundred denarii and given to the poor?" he argued.[6] His argument and the tone of his voice seemed to be an overreaction. He argued, not because he cared that much for the poor, but because he was a petty thief and had been stealing from the money box he carried.[7] Now his words revealed his true motives.

Still reclined and appreciating the actions of Mary, Jesus rebuked Judas. "Leave her alone. She has done a beautiful thing." Sternly fixing his

---

4   Mark 14:3
5   Joshua 15:25
6   A denarii was about a day's wage, so this perfume was equivalent to a year's wage, a further indication of the wealth and position of Lazarus and his sisters.
7   John 12:6; John 13:29

Anointed for Burial

eyes on Judas he said, "The poor you have with you always and whenever you want, you can do good for them."

Then Jesus announced to the crowd, "She has anointed my body beforehand for burial."[8] The Lord was well aware of how this week would end, and he was reminded of it by this anointing. How ironic that when he died on the cross, there would not be time to anoint his body properly before he was placed in the tomb. Whenever the gospel story is told, Mary will forever be famous as the only one who properly anointed him for his burial.[9]

But Jesus' rebuke sank deep into the heart of Judas. "Why did he rebuke me so harshly? Does he know what I've been doing?" All during the night his guilty conscious could not escape the thought. "I've been found out. What will Jesus do? What will the other men do if Jesus tells them?" It was a restless night for Judas. In the darkness, his greed opened up the door to his soul, and Satan entered in.[10]

---

8   John 12:7,
9   Mark 14:9
10 John 13:2

Chapter Five

Sunday's Triumphal Entry

> "When He approached Jerusalem,
> He saw the city and wept over it..."
>
> Luke 19:41

It was a beautiful spring Sunday morning in Bethany as the Lord awoke and rose to face the day. This would be his day; his day to claim his birthright to the throne of David; his day to be welcomed as the rightful King of Israel with all its symbolic and prophetic meaning. It was to be the day he would be inaugurated as a king of a kingdom "not of this world."[1] This day would overwhelm his enemies and excite the multitudes. It was the first day of the week, a day that would become known for all time as

---

1 John 18:36

"the Lord's day."

On the other hand, the Apostles awoke to a day they feared would be trouble, big trouble! They began to gather around Lazarus' home in anticipation of what they felt would certainly be a dangerous day in Jerusalem. Other disciples also gathered, as well as many pilgrims who had stayed on this far hillside of Olivet. As Jesus - the Master, the teacher, the miracle worker - gathered his forces together, the word quickly spread toward Jerusalem announcing his coming. Those who had been eye witnesses of Lazarus' resurrection testified to what they had seen, which further motivated many out-of-town visitors to want to see Jesus.[2] Soon they were rushing out from Jerusalem and Bethphage on the west and Bethany on the east.[3] Just before Jesus began to walk from one side of the Mount of Olives to the other, toward Jerusalem, he called out two of his disciples[4] with a special mission. They were to go ahead into the little hamlet of Bethphage, and there fetch a young donkey colt and meet him with it. If the owners asked any questions, he instructed them to reply, "The Lord has need of it." [5]

As the crowds began to make their way toward Jesus, the scene became one of joy and excitement. "The Talk of the Town" was coming to town. Most of the crowds were pilgrims who had come from great

---

2   John 12:17
3   On the Mount of Olivet were three places of importance in the Gospels. The mount itself was directly opposite Mount Zion, where the temple and city of Jerusalem stood. Between the two mounts was the Kidron Valley. On the western slope of the Mount of Olives was the Garden of Gethsemane, (the grove of olive trees where Jesus loved to rest) and the little village of Bethphage. On the eastern slope of the Mount was Bethany, less than two miles from Jerusalem.
4   While the text does not give us the names of the "two disciples" Jesus sent to get the colt, we know that Jesus often called on Peter and John for special tasks, and some assume the same here. See Luke 22:8; compare Acts 3:1.
5   Mark 11:1-3

"Behold Your King Is Coming To You."

distances, who had never seen Jesus, but had heard of his famous miracles and his messianic teachings. They were looking for some excitement and Jesus was just the ticket! In the midst of this mass exodus going out to see Jesus, the two disciples arrived in Bethphage and spotted the young donkey tied beside its mother. As they began to untie it, the owner came forward and asked what they were doing. "The Lord has need of it," they properly responded. The owner, himself aware of Jesus' imminent arrival, seemed pleased that he could somehow be of service to the Lord, and gladly released the young colt to the two disciples. To encourage the young animal to go with them, its mother was also untied and led away.[6]

Now somewhere atop the hillside of Olivet, a great and awesome convergence occurred. Jesus and his followers from Bethany met the crowds from Jerusalem and Bethphage.[7] At the same time the donkey colt arrived. Some of Jesus' men took off their robes and threw them over the small animal and Jesus took his seat upon its back. The young donkey had never been ridden before, yet it did not buck, or balk. It seemed the Lord had control over more in nature than just the wind.

Jesus was to be a different kind of king, as his steed illustrated. He was not David arriving with his mighty soldiers from some great conquest, or Solomon entering the city in his shining chariot drawn by majestic war horses. Jesus came fulfilling the prophet's words;

---

6   Matthew 21:2-7; Matthew indicates that both animals were fetched according to Jesus' instruction. We do not know what happened to the mother, but it would be safe to assume that she remained in the procession, perhaps lost in the crowds at times.
7   Mark 11:1; John 12:12

Sunday's Triumphal Entry

"Shout in triumph, O daughter of Jerusalem!
 Behold, your king is coming to you;
He is just and endowed with salvation,
Humble, and mounted on a donkey,
Even on a colt, the foal of a donkey."[8]

The small colt slowly walked forward with Israel's savior upon its back. The Apostles watched in amazement as the crowds began to remove their robes and laid them in the path of the Lord, forming a momentary carpet. Others cut off the branches of the palm trees around and spread them before the path of the advancing king. As the crowds grew, the noise of their jubilation drifted across the Kidron valley and could be heard all the way to the temple. His Apostles were completely taken aback by the welcome. They had been fearful of his coming to Jerusalem, and now to see the whole city give him such a king-like greeting was overwhelming and even confusing to them. Their worried faces gave way to nervous smiles. It would be some time later before they would reflect on this day and come to understand it all.[9]

Coming out of the city and rushing up the hillside were some of the Pharisees who had come to see what all the commotion was about. They were astonished and disheartened by what they saw. After their "arrest" announcements and all of their threats, "he gets a welcome like this?" In anger they began to point accusing fingers at each other, "You see that you are not doing any good," one taunted the other. Throwing up their

---

8 Zechariah 9:9; John 12:15
9 John 12:16

Road To The Upper Room

hands in frustration they complained to one another, "Look! The whole world has gone after him!"[10]

As Jesus began to top the hillside and inch his way down the rocky path, the shouts filled the air, "Hosanna! Blessed is he who comes in the name of the Lord!" The shouts grew louder, "Blessed is the coming kingdom of our father David!" Then the cries of the multitudes began to echo across the Kidron valley, off the temple walls, and into the Holy of Holies, "Hosanna in the highest!" "Blessed is the King who comes in the name of the Lord." This moment was the Law's fulfillment, the Lord's vindication, and the Pharisee's worst nightmare.

In a moment of total desperation some of the Pharisees pushed their way through the adoring crowd, rushed up to Jesus, and begged him to rebuke his disciples, to bring this celebration to an end. With quick wit and a bit of righteous indignation Jesus replied, "I tell you if these become silent, the stones will cry out!"[11]

Jesus nudged his donkey forward, and as he reached a certain place on the hillside of Mount Olivet, the city of Jerusalem came into full view across the valley. It was one of the most impressive cities on the face of the earth, situated on the tall hill of Mount Zion. Jesus gazed upon the gold columns and temple tower, the impressive wall, and the palace of Herod, all framed by the surrounding gardens and wealthy homes. As he slid off the colt and looked upon the City of David, tears begin to roll down his cheeks. In his mind's eye he was not seeing the city's beauty, but its sin; not its greatness, but its rejection of God's Messiah. He knew

10 John 12:19
11 John 19:39-40

of the city's future destruction, and the death and horror which would come. The jubilation of the moment was now dissolved by the Lord's heavy sobs and laments. "Oh Jerusalem, Jerusalem!" he cried out. "The days will come upon you when your enemies will throw up a barricade against you," he proclaimed, "and they will level you to the ground and your children within you, and they will not leave in you one stone upon another, because you did not recognize and welcome God's personal visit."[12]

As the young donkey colt and its mother were led back to its owners, Jesus led the crowds down the valley, up into the city, and toward the temple gates. In his first action as king, he had some house cleaning to do.

---

12   Luke 19:42-44; The last part of this verse was taken from The Message translation. This prophesies came true in AD 70 when Rome came and destroyed Jerusalem, killing a million of its inhabitants.

Chapter Six

Cleansing the Temple Again

> *"And He said to them, 'It was written,*
> *"My house shall be called a house of Prayer"';*
> *but you are making it a robbers' den."*
>
> Matthew 21:13

By the time Jesus arrived at Jerusalem's great gates, the entire city was stirred up. It appeared that the Pharisees' statement rang true: the whole world had gone after him! Up the slope of mighty Mount Zion the Rod of Judah walked with ten thousand admirers rushing ahead announcing his coming and another ten thousand behind shouting his praises.[1] Jesus' Twelve crowded around him. They intensely looked about the crowds,

---

1   Farrar, page 334: states, "The dense crowd of Jews- numbering, it was said, three million, crowded into the holy city during the week of the feast."

still in shock and disbelief at the reception of their Master, being themselves moved along by the swell of people.

Jesus entered the city on the east, walked through the priests-suburb of Ophel and then through and up one of the two tunneled stairs of the Huldah gates, which opened up into the immense area of Solomon's Colonnade, a huge courtyard that could accommodate over two hundred thousand visitors.[2] He was anxious to find a suitable place to huddle the people around him and spend the remainder of the day teaching and healing his devoted audience. But as he walked across the great Gentile court and through the gate called Beautiful into the temple proper, he was dismayed by what he saw. When he was last there in December, the temple was decorated with thousands of candles showing off the glory of this magnificent structure, forty-six years in the making. It was clean and beautiful like a bride dressed for her wedding day.

Now as he entered he heard the bleating of sheep and smelled the stench of dung. Everywhere he looked there were row after row of tables where the money changers and merchants had set up shop. Some were buying, some were selling. He walked past hastily erected pens holding cattle and lambs, and benches filled with small cages of doves. As he walked, his anger and disgust grew. He had seen this before. He had cleansed the temple of this filth and greed three years ago.[3] But the merchants had returned. To their dismay, so had Jesus. In righteous indignation he turned over one table and then another. Coins began to scatter upon the temple pavement. Bankers grabbed their money, sellers

---

2   Edersheim;The Temple, p 114
3   John 2:13-16

Cleansing The Temple Again

jumped, doves flew from overturned cages. The first time Jesus had used a whip to chase them out, but now with the authority of a newly crowned king, and with the massive crowds behind him, he moved down the court disrupting one business after another. He shouted orders to his loyal subjects, "Do not let even a basket of goods enter the temple!"[4] He could not run them all out, and under the watchful eye of the Roman tower, he must not make too big of a commotion. Yet he would certainly make his point.

Stepping to the top of the staircase, he stood before the pillars and his voice filled the great expanse of the temple court. It was a voice that had taught with authority, a voice which had stopped soldiers in their tracks, a voice that now rang strong and clear across the courtyard and into the Holy Place, "It is written: 'My house will be called a house of prayer for all nations, but you have made it a den of thieves!'"[5]

The priests watching from above in their lofty perch overlooking the temple grounds were infuriated. They received income from the merchants in the temple. Their big week of revenue was being disrupted before their very eyes. In truth, they were the object of Jesus' rebuke. They were the ones who had turned this holy week into a carnival atmosphere and the temple of God into a marketplace. On this day Jesus struck a symbolic, if not heavy, blow against his biggest opponents - the Pharisees and the high priest. But in their anger they could only sit and watch as

---

4   Mark 11:16
5   Matthew 21:12-17; Mark 11:15-17; Luke 19:45-46 While Matthew and Luke show the cleansing of the temple to take place on Sunday, after the triumphal entry, Mark places it on Monday after the fig tree was cursed. John makes no mention of the event. It seems that Mark was inclined to tie the judgment of Jesus upon the fig tree to the judgment he renders against the moneychangers. In this case I think the majority rules and we must leave the cleansing of the temple in its proper chronology- on Sunday. I agree with such great writers as Farrar that effectually argue in favor of the Sunday scenario. Quite frankly, when the events of Monday are considered, it seems difficult to see this cleansing taking place on Monday morning.

many of the money changers carried their goods outside the temple and several shepherds gathered up their flocks and moved out into the less hostile hillside. The priests watched as the crowds then assembled by the thousands around Jesus as he began to teach and heal.

They had lost control of the temple grounds. They looked down from their quarters on the second floor of the portico and could only murmur under their breath. To add insult to injury, they watched as the children assembled before Jesus and began to lift their sweet voices in praise, proclaiming "Hosanna to the Son of David."[6] The religious elite wanted so badly to get rid of this man, to see him dead, but after the events of this day they could only look at each other in frustration. At this moment they were afraid of him! [7]

At the end of this monumental day Jesus left the temple to head back to Bethany. As he departed, he turned and took one long look at this great structure.[8] It was here he came as a young boy and first saw through human eyes his Father's house. It was where he first discussed God's Law, and where he would soon teach his last. He gazed upon its beauty in the evening light with its gold shimmering upon the majestic columns. For a brief moment he focused upon the great altar where many animals had been sacrificed for the sins of the people; he knew that soon another sacrifice must take place.

It was now four days before the Passover.

---

6   Matthew 21:15-16
7   Mark 11:18
8   Mark 11:11

Chapter Seven
Monday's Quiet Day

> *"Now My soul has become troubled; and what shall I say, 'Father, save Me from this hour'? But for this purpose I came to this hour."*
>
> John 12:27

The next morning,[1] with the excitement of the previous day behind him, Jesus was ready to return to the temple for some serious time of teaching and healing. With the comfort of Lazarus' home available to him, he had preferred to spend much of the night in fasting and prayer. Knowing of things that were about to come to pass, he needed this time to talk to his Father.

---

1   John 12:12

Road To The Upper Room

With little sleep, Jesus rose early[2] and assembled those who were ready to go with him. As they began the two-mile walk in the early hours of Monday morning, he heard his stomach growling. He was hungry and ready to break his fast.[3]

On the journey he saw a fig tree nearby, standing alone. It was in full leaf, meaning that figs should be there.[4] As his disciples watched, Jesus walked over and began to pull the leaves back looking for some fruit to alleviate his hunger. There was none. Leaf after leaf the Lord looked, and with each moment became more disappointed with this fruitless tree. After his thorough examination of the fig tree, Jesus stepped back and pronounced a judgment upon this plant, "May no one ever eat fruit from you again!" His disciples all heard this judgment. As they continued the journey, Matthew was the last to pass by and was startled to see that the tree had already begun to wither.[5]

The fig tree was a symbol of Israel. And now in the full leaf of the Passover feast, God's beloved people appeared to be a healthy spiritual tree. But as God came down and walked among them He had not found the fruit of righteousness that He craved. This city would soon be under God's curse and in the darkness of a coming noon. In that darkness Israel, like the fig tree, would begin to wither from its leadership down.

This event set a negative tone for the day ahead. The disciples were

---

2   Luke 21:38
3   Matthew 21:18, Mark 11:12-13; Known for her hospitality, it was difficult to conceive that Martha would have allowed Jesus to go through the night, and leave out in the morning, without a proper meal. Yet, for some reason Jesus had not eaten. In difficult times he often would spend much of the night in fasting and prayer (see Luke 6:12; Luke 11:1; Matthew 14:23). Coffman also expresses this same thought: Commentary on Matthew 21:18
4   The fig tree was a unique plant, bearing its fruit first, then its leaves.
5   Matthew 21:19

The Fruitless Fig Tree

Road To The Upper Room

a bit taken aback by this as they were somewhat relieved by the king's welcome he received the day before. Perhaps the danger was past they thought. Yet Jesus knew better, and knew how strongly he was being rejected by the Jewish leaders. His soul was troubled as he moved toward the city and the sound of the Roman soldier's hammer began to ring louder in his ears.

Jesus completed the familiar journey down Olivet's slope, across the valley of Kidron, and up into the city just a few hundred feet from where diverted springs flowed through Hezekiah's tunnel and emptied its waters into the pool of Siloam. Jesus entered the temple once again up the tunneled staircase which led into the Gentiles' court within the temple grounds. Keeping a lower profile, he milled through the crowds, talking with well-wishers, disciples, and the many visitors from out of town. Finding a nice spot in the early morning sunlight, he took his seat, and as the crowd gathered around he began conversing with them at first, and then moved into the lesson of the day.[6]

His twelve Apostles did not always shadow him, but some made their own journeys through the crowds, visiting with family and friends, and enjoying the excitement of the Passover festivities. Some in Philip's family had made acquaintances with some Gentile visitors who had come to worship. They heard of this great prophet and inquired where they could

---

6   Luke 21:37-38

find him. They were introduced to Philip and made this simple request, "Sir, we wish to see Jesus."[7]

Philip would not grant such an audience without consulting with some of the other men. Out of respect for their Master, and in view of the many requests that came their way, each request had to be carefully considered before bothering Jesus with it. So Philip conferred with Andrew and they decided to grant these Greeks the audience they had come so far to have. At an appropriate moment in the Lord's morning, he informed Jesus of the Greeks' request.

Jesus used their desire to see him to contrast the rejection he had received from Israel's leaders, and to speak of the death that his own people would bring upon him. "The hour has come for the Son of Man to be glorified," he announced. No more fleeing the temple mobs; no more journeys to Ephraim to escape the Pharisees' threats. His hour was near.

"Truly, truly, I say to you, unless a grain of wheat falls into the earth and dies, it remains alone; but if it dies, it bears much fruit." Then lifting his eyes heavenward he prayed, "Father, glorify your name." Immediately a great voice sounded from the heavens, "I have both glorified it, and will glorify it again!" God himself had spoken for the last time from the Holy of Holies.

"Thunder!" some in the crowd shouted. "No," cried others. "It was the voice of an angel."

---

[7] John 12:20-21 Only John records this incident and Jesus' response. A key event in understanding the chronology of Monday and Tuesday is the fig tree. We know Jesus cursed it on Monday and its withered condition was noticed on Tuesday. Since all of the texts of Matthew, Mark, and Luke were clearly tied to Tuesday, and they make no mention of the visit of the Greeks as does John, we were left to conclude with some degree of confidence, that this text records the only event of Monday. True to John's unique gospel, this was the only event he records that took place on Monday and/or Tuesday.

Road To The Upper Room

Jesus responded, "It was a voice meant for you to let you know that judgment was about to begin, and the evil in the world was going to be overthrown." Accepting that his hour had come and referring to the type of death that was coming with it, he proclaimed, "And I, if I am lifted up from the earth, will draw all men to myself."[8]

The dramatic effect of God's voice thundering over the temple crowd caused quite a stir, and Jesus, his heart now heavy with the shadow of the cross looming ever darker over him,[9] withdrew from the crowd and remained hidden from them the rest of the day.[10]

Also in hiding throughout the day were the chief priest, scribes, and the elders of the city; all of whom were either of the party of Pharisees or Sadducees. They remained perplexed about how to deal with Jesus, but had decided upon a plan which they would put into action when he came to the temple the next day.

---

8   John 12:27-33
9   John 12:27
10   John 12:36

Chapter Eight

Tuesday's Confrontations

"But woe to you, scribes and Pharisees, hypocrites..."
Matthew 23:13

As the sun lightened the eastern sky, the roosters of Bethany began to announce the arrival of Tuesday morning. It was now two days before the Passover. Jesus emerged from the front door of Lazarus' home to find that several of his Apostles had already gathered. They knew Jesus would want to leave early for Jerusalem. Some latecomers would have to catch up, while one or two would be waiting to join them along the way. It would prove to be a very long day.

Road To The Upper Room

Peter's voice broke the morning silence. "Rabbi, look, the fig tree which you cursed has withered." The group stopped to gaze upon the tree and saw that it did not just appear sickly, but its leaves and even its roots had shriveled up. A freshly hewn tree might still appear green and healthy for several days. Not so with this fruitless and cursed tree. Within a day it had been reduced to a twisted piece of dried-up wood.

"Have faith in God," Jesus encouraged his men as they paused to stare at what remained of this poor tree. Standing on the top of the mountain Olivet, Jesus gazed out and caught a glimmer of the Dead Sea, several miles away and 2300 feet below them, then he continued with his morning object lesson. "Whoever says to this mountain, 'Be taken up and cast into the sea' and does not doubt in his heart, but believes what he says was going to happen, it will be granted him."[1]

Having received their first lesson of the morning they moved on toward the city, and the temple of God. Entering, Jesus began to walk about to find a suitable place to teach for the morning.[2] Awaiting his arrival, the chief priests, scribes, and elders immediately began to follow him. They would not sit quietly by as they had the day before. Their plan was to disrupt his day, embarrass him if they could, and regain control of the temple and its crowds. Jesus found a familiar place atop one of the many elevated steps in Solomon's Porch and sat. His sitting indicated to the crowds that he was ready to teach, so they quickly gathered around and he began to speak.[3] Immediately some of the priests stepped forward and interrupted;

"Tell us by what authority you are doing these things," they asked in

---
1   Mark 11:20-26
2   Mark 11:27
3   Matthew 21:23

reference to his disruption of the money changers, and the healing of the sick. "Or who gave you this authority?"[4]

Jesus stood to face them squarely and replied, "I will also ask you a question and you tell me: Was the baptism of John from heaven or from men?"

Now confronted by their own mischief, and facing the intense gaze of the crowd, they huddled together and whispered among themselves, "If we say, 'from heaven,' he will say, 'Why did you not believe him?'" Another whispers, "But yet if we say, 'from men,' all the people will stone us to death, for they are convinced that John was a prophet."

Breaking the huddle, they sheepishly faced the Lord and the crowd, as their spokesman was urged forward and announced, "We do not know where John's authority came from?"

"Then neither will I tell you by what authority I do these things," Jesus said as he stepped ever closer to them so as not to allow them to escape the moment.

Embarrassed and fearing the glaring gaze of the crowd, the priests, elders, and scribes slithered back into the shadows of the colonnade. But Jesus was not about to let them leave just yet. He and the crowd moved forward toward them. The wrath of God's Son had just begun to come down upon their heads. With their backs against the wall in more ways than one, they had to listen as Jesus spoke, "Truly I say that the tax collectors and prostitutes will get into the kingdom of God before you. For you did not believe John, but the tax collectors and prostitutes did believe him! Therefore I tell you that the kingdom of God will be taken

---

4   Matthew 21:23-32; Mark 11:27-33

away from you and given to a people who will produce its fruit."[5] As he spoke there was a withered tree across the valley that learned too well the consequences of fruitlessness in the face of God.

With hatred for this man burning in their hearts, they escaped back to the safety of their meeting hall. "We must have him arrested!" some suggested. But that idea quickly died as they looked out and saw the magnitude of the crowds about him, hanging on to his every word.[6] "Some believe him to be a prophet." [7] For a moment there was silence, but they were not about to give up.

They decided to continue their tactics. First, a group of Pharisees confronted him about paying taxes to Caesar. Jesus answered, "Render unto Caesar the things that are Caesar's, and unto God the things that are God's."[8] They could only shake their heads in amazement and call it a day.[9] Next the Sadducees gave it their best shot. "A woman was married to a man who had seven brothers," they stated. "Her husband died and she married one of his brothers, and he died, and this happened until she had married all seven brothers and they all had died, and then she died." Now they had their trap set. "In the resurrection, therefore, whose wife of the seven will she be for they all had married her?" An interesting approach since the Sadducees did not even believe in a resurrection.[10]

Jesus' reply was swift and crushing. "You are wrong on two counts because you do not know your Scriptures, nor the power of God. For in

---

5 Matthew 21:43
6 Luke 19:48
7 Matthew 21:46
8 Matthew 22:15-21
9 Matthew 22:22
10 Acts 23:8

Road To The Upper Room

the resurrection there is neither marriage nor giving to marriage, but we are like the angels in heaven."[11] The answer astonished the crowd and left the Sadducees speechless.

Finally, a lawyer made his way to the front and tried his hand at questioning, but to no avail.[12] Lacking the courage to go on,[13] they decided to give up on this tactic.[14]

But the carpenter of Nazareth was not finished speaking to the multitudes, and in view of the religious leaders' vicious attempts to trap him throughout the morning, he decided to release a tirade against them that they would forever remember. As some of these scribes and Pharisees stood in the back of the massive crowds, and others peered down from their upper-room windows in Solomon's Colonnade, Jesus spoke, "These religious men study Moses' law, so what they teach you about that law you need to obey; but do not follow their examples, because they do not obey their own teachings."

"They load you down with heavy rules that they themselves do not follow."

"They love to sit at the head of the table and be called by their fancy titles out in the market.

"But woe to you scribes and Pharisees, you are nothing but hypocrites! You force widows out of their houses by fraud and then stand in the marketplace and act holy by praying some long prayer. Woe to you scribes, Pharisees; hypocrites!"

11	Matthew 22:23-33
12	Matthew 22:34-40
13	Luke 20:40
14	Matthew 22:46

Pointing out over the crowd to these very men he continued, "You fools and blind guides! You lead some Gentile to the law then destroy his soul by making him just like yourselves."

"You pull a few leaves off your spice plants and give them in tithe, but then conveniently leave undone the weightier provisions of the law. Your tithing is good, but you neglect justice and mercy and faithfulness. You blind guides; you strain out a gnat and swallow a camel!"

"Woe to you, scribes and Pharisees, hypocrites! You are like the whitewashed tombs which on the outside appear beautiful, but inside are full of dead men's bones and all uncleanness. You too appear righteous on the outside with your fancy robes and broad phylacteries, but in your heart you are full of hypocrisy and lawlessness! You serpents, you brood of vipers, how will you escape the sentence of hell?" [15]

Leaving his foes to grind their teeth, Jesus walked across the courtyard, through the gate called Beautiful, and took a seat inside the court of Women. There, surrounded by his twelve Apostles, he sat quietly, letting his spirit calm down as he watched those who were coming and going.

But the Jewish leaders were not sitting quietly. His stunning rebuke was the last straw. With the truth of his words burning in their consciences, and with their reputations all but destroyed, they gathered in small groups around the temple grounds, out of the glaring sight of the multitudes. Word began to spread that there would be a meeting shortly across town at the house of Caiaphas, the high priest.[16] His courtyard would give them the privacy they needed to address such a serious tongue-lashing.

---

15 Matthew 23:1-33; Mark 12:38-40
16 Matthew 26:3

Road To The Upper Room

Their sacred temple and beautiful meeting hall had become unfriendly territory because of the ranting of this crazy carpenter and his little band of Galileans.

Chapter Nine

The Final Teachings

> *"As He was going out of the temple, one of His disciples said to Him, 'Teacher, behold what wonderful stones and what wonderful buildings.'"*
>
> Mark 13:1

As Jesus sat just inside the main entrance to the temple proper, in the Court of Women near the gate called Beautiful, he watched as people put their money into the temple treasury. The treasury was a collection of thirteen different boxes, narrow at the mouth and wide at the bottom, giving them the name of "trumpets."[1] They all sat in one area close to the gate and each trumpet had its own unique purpose. Trumpet boxes one and two were for the temple tribute, trumpet three and four for the

---

1   Edersheim, The Temple; page 25-26

Road To The Upper Room

dove sacrifices of the poor, trumpet five for the wood of the temple, and number six for the incense, and so on. Jesus had played upon the word when he described the conduct of those who, in their almsgiving sought the glory of men and so "sounded the trumpet" in which they made their donation.[2]

With the tens of thousands of visitors in the city, each coming with a temple offering, the line to the treasury was a long one. Jesus watched as many were proudly making their deposits. His attention focused on an elderly lady moving along slowly toward the trumpet-shaped boxes. His keen eye noticed as she took coins from her purse, two small copper coins, and dropped them in the treasury to pay for her dove sacrifice. "This poor widow has put in more than all of them," he noted, "for they all out of their surplus put into the offering, but she out of her poverty put in all that she had to live on."[3]

As Judas Iscariot took all this in, his heart was hardened by Jesus' words as he looked with envy upon the wealth of those "sounding the trumpet." Soon thirty pieces of silver from this same treasury would be in his pocket.

At last it was time to go. Jesus knew as he was leaving the temple, and the great city of David, that his public ministry had come to an end. The joy of the blind receiving their sight within its walls would be no more. The great crowds that had surrounded him each day would soon turn against him. One of his own was about to betray him. The events would soon transpire that would cause John later to write:

2   Matthew 6:2
3   Luke 21:1-4

The Final Teachings

"He came to his own,

And those who were His own did not receive Him"[4]

As he went out he cried a lament; "Oh Jerusalem, Jerusalem, who kill the prophets and stone those who were sent to her. How often I wanted to gather your chickens together, the way a hen gathers her chicks under her wings, and you were unwilling. Behold your house is being left to you desolate!"[5]

Out of the city, striding up Olivet's slope, one of his Apostles turned to point out just how beautiful and magnificent Herod's great building was. Unlike Lot's wife, Jesus had no desire to look back, and his response was unexpected as he strode up the slope toward Gethsemane; "Truly I say to you not one stone here will be left upon another, which will not be torn down."[6]

Across the valley, and within the city walls, the meeting at Caiaphas' house was getting underway.

Arriving in the garden of olive trees known as Gethsemane, Jesus brought his journey to a halt. As they sat, or lay about, in restful contemplation, they discussed the future of Jerusalem in light of the Lord's statements. One of them, the one who would betray him, was taking note of how often the Lord had brought them there. Peter, James, John, and Andrew began to question Jesus privately, "Tell us, when will these things will be?"[7]

4   John 1:11
5   Matthew 23:37-38
6   Matthew 24:1-2; in less than forty years Jesus prediction would come true. The Jews rebelled against Rome and the emperor Vespasian sent his army which destroyed Jerusalem and the temple. More than a million Jews who had crowded into the city, perished. As a government Israel ceased to exist. The "fig tree" had withered from its roots up.
7   Mark 13:3-4

Road To The Upper Room

Over the next couple of hours Jesus gave some of the greatest lessons of his ministry. As he began to speak to his audience of four on the Mount of Olives, he warned them of the treatment they would receive after he was gone. "Be on your guard; for they will deliver you to the courts, and you will be flogged in the synagogues, and you will stand before governors and kings for my sake. You will be hated by all because of my name, but the one who endures to the end will be saved."[8]

Beneath the twisted limbs of the great olive trees, the others began to gather around as Jesus spoke of the destruction that would come upon Israel. He warned of false Christs and false prophets that would arise after his departure. He spoke of his own return. He expressed their need to be faithful and ready through the parables that would become some of his most memorable. In the parable of the fig tree when he said, "But of that day and hour no one knows, not even the angels of heaven, nor the Son, but the Father alone"[9] In the parable of the ten virgins, he taught about wise and foolish preparation.[10]

He followed this with the parable of the talents in which a servant hid his Master's silver and was thrown into outer darkness, where there was "weeping and gnashing of teeth."[11] Finally, he described the last great Judgment Day when the Son of Man would separate the sheep from the goats.

Jesus' words were spoken with a tone that reflected a deeply troubled spirit. There was sadness in his voice as they prepared to leave this be-

8	Mark 13:9-13
9	Matthew 24:24-51
10	Matthew 25:1-13
11	Matthew 25:14-30

loved garden and return to Bethany. "You know," he said, "that after two days the Passover is coming, and the Son of Man is to be handed over for crucifixion." [12]

Arising, they walked from Gethsemane's shadows to return to Bethany. His ministry had now come to an end. All that remained was for the Passover lamb to be slain.

---

[12]   Matthew 25:31-26:2

Chapter Ten
In Caiaphas' Courtyard

"Then the chief priests and the elders of the people were gathered together in the court of the high priest named Caiaphas; and they plotted together to seize Jesus by stealth and kill Him."

Matthew 26: 3-4

Caiaphas was a ruthless man, and capable of doing whatever needed to be done in order to hold on to power and have his own way. Even kill. He was the son-in-law of Annas, who was high priest from A.D. 6-15. Caiaphas had been appointed high priest by Pilate's predecessor, and would hold that position until A.D. 36.

In the meeting held when they heard that Jesus had raised Lazarus from the dead, it was Caiaphas who said it would be "expedient" for one man to die in order for "Israel" to survive.[1] It was by Caiaphas' leadership that the Sanhedrin council officially began to plan Jesus' death.[2] This high priest was the embodiment of that whitewashed tomb Jesus had proclaimed was full of hypocrisy and lawlessness. Caiaphas could have ended all this animosity toward Jesus. He could have stopped the Pharisees' attacks; he could have examined honestly the claims made by the prophet of Nazareth. He chose not to. Rather, out of envy for Jesus' true power and popularity, he sought his death.[3]

Now to Caiaphas' courtyard they came; away from the crowds that they feared and still stinging from the accusing voice of their adversary. They knew that they could not overcome Jesus in public debate, so they needed to resort to their strength - secret schemes. Months before, they decided to kill him and now they just needed to figure out a way to do it. If only they could come up with some sly trick that he would fall for, some subtle plan that would catch him off guard. So far everything had failed. They needed a break, such as one of his disciples to come forth with a complaint they might use to build a case. Or, perhaps one of his own would turn against him. They could only hope and wait.

After lengthy discussion, and to their frustration, no suitable plan was devised. The meeting adjourned with only one real decision - they must wait until the Passover feast was over, when the crowds were gone, so as to avoid some riot over his arrest.[4] As they were deciding to postpone the slaying of the Lord, at that very moment, seated under the evening shade

---

1   John 11:47, 50; 18:14
2   John 11:47, 53
3   Matthew 27:18
4   Matthew 26:4-5

In Caiaphas' Courtyard

of Gethsemane's giant limbs, Jesus was instructing his disciples that he would indeed be slain as the Passover lamb.

Now, in the evening light of a warm spring day, two groups of men gathered. One group gathered within the privacy of gray stone walls, the other under the shade of great olive trees. One group met under the happy smile of the Prince of Darkness, the other under the sorrowful gaze of the God of Heaven. One man led his followers in a plan to kill, while another prepared his men to accept God's will. One group walked home through the shadows of the temple's wall, the other over Olivet's crest past a withered fig tree.

It was now two days before the Passover.

The Narrative

Section Three:
The Last Day

Chapter One
Thirty Pieces of Silver

> *"And he went away and discussed with the chief priests and officers how he might betray Him to them. They were glad and agreed to give him money."*
>
> Luke 22:4, 5

It was a restless night for Judas Iscariot. Over and over in his mind he weighed the feelings of Caiaphas and the Pharisees toward Jesus and considered his own position. Somewhere in the darkness he made the final decision to betray his master. The Evil One helped him rationalize his actions. After all, Jesus had spoken of his own death and had told them that those who followed him could lose their lives as well. He warned them of how they would be arrested and beaten. Judas wanted no part of this. Then there was the fear that Jesus would reveal Judas' own greed and theft from the group's money. How would the other men react to this? Had his ill-gotten source of income come to an end? All of this was too much for him to endure. He had seen how much the Jewish leaders hated Jesus; perhaps he could cash in one last time and then disappear.

All of Jesus' twelve Apostles had their faults and weaknesses. It was to Jesus' credit that he took twelve men such as these and molded and shaped them into a group of men who would take his message and change the world. He often chided them for their faults and lack of faith. As each man failed, the Lord drew him back with loving cords. They became penitent and came back stronger. How many times had Peter disappointed the Lord, yet humbly saw his weakness and grew stronger? The shocking tragedy of Judas' life was not his thievery, but his impenitence. He listened to the Lord's words, saw his miracles, experienced his tenderness, yet the call of the money box and his own personal fears and insecurity won the day. And Satan was there to hold his hand.

Wednesday morning was the perfect time to put his plan into action. It was a day of preparation when all leaven was to be cleared from the home. This began the preparations for the eight days of unleavened bread.[1] Every home would throw out any leaven and scrub and clean everything in the house that may have come in contact with it. Many of the shops in the city would close early, if they opened at all, to allow owners to return to their homes and do the necessary cleansing by sunset[2]. Any needs Jesus' group still had for the Passover would have to be purchased

---

1   Exodus 12:15-20
2   Edersheim; *The Temple*, chapter 9, p. 553

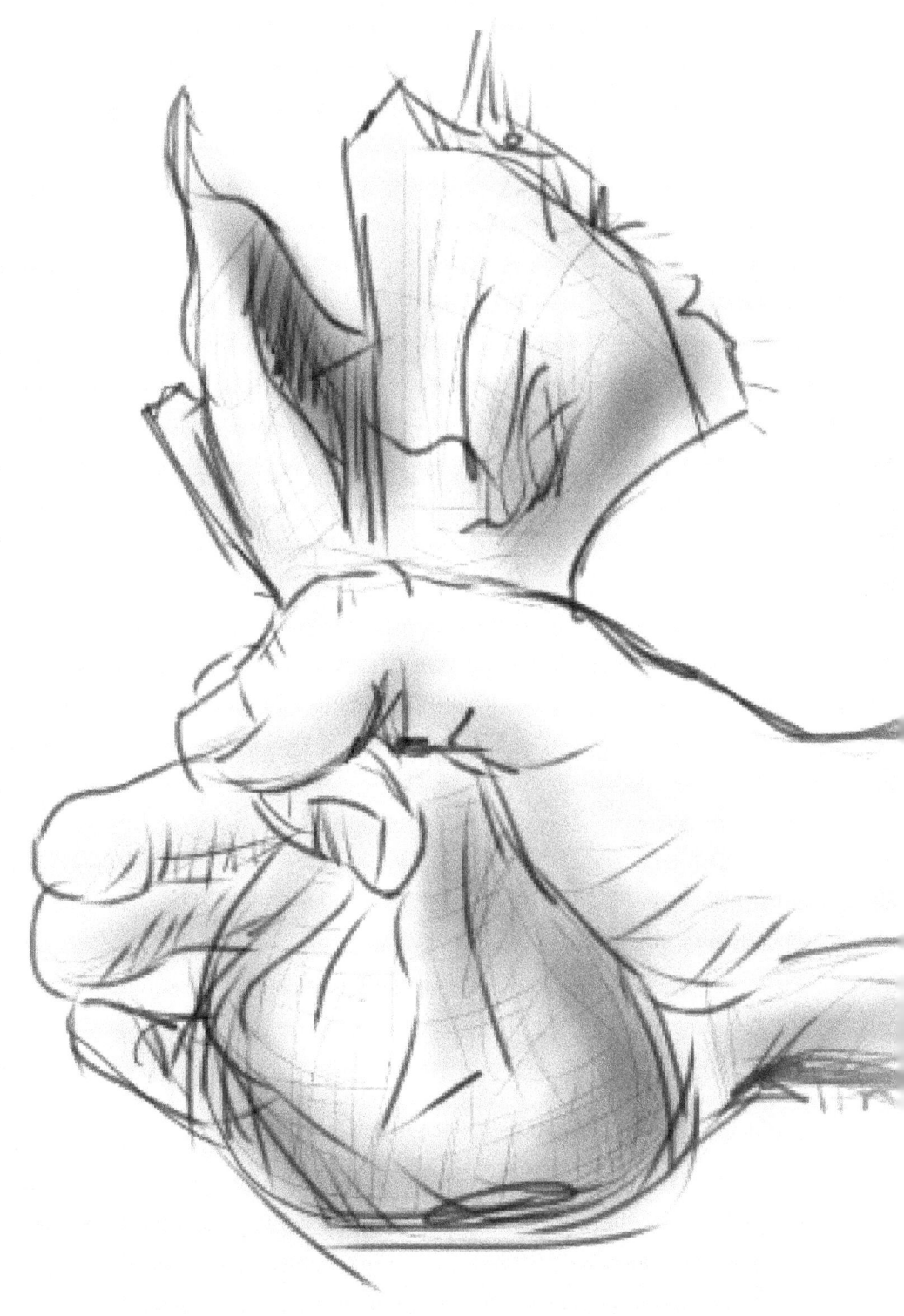

"They Weight Unto Him 30 Pieces Of Silver."

that morning, and if the lamb had not yet been paid for, this too would need to be done. The temple grounds would be cleared and the gates closed around midday to allow the Levites time to prepare the temple for the Passover. Many additional altars would have to be set up in preparation for the massive slayings of the Passover lambs the next day.[3]

In view of these events, Jesus would not be going into the city. He would instead stay in Bethany and spend the day in quiet meditation. Judas was able to go into town that morning without raising suspicion with the real need to purchase items for the Passover or to tend to other personal matters.

On this beautiful spring morning, Judas entered Jerusalem and quickly completed his errands. He then made his way past the shops and bakeries, around one corner and then another, walking upon the stone-paved streets and beneath the rock archways until he found himself standing in front of the house of the high priest. On this important and busy day, many of the chief priests and members of the Sanhedrin were there. Judas identified himself to the temple officers and requested a meeting with the resident of the house, the high priest Caiaphas.

As Judas entered the majestic residence some of the priests and elders recognized him as "one of the twelve."[4] A few knew him vaguely as he was a Judean, not a Galilean like the other eleven. A quiet murmur began to float around the room as his position was quickly identified and their curiosity rose.

After some introductions and small talk, Judas got to the point. He

---

3   Josephus estimated that at the A.D. 70 Passover …"the number of sacrifices was two hundred and fifty-six thousand five hundred." Broadhurst, p. 43
4   Matthew 26:14

Thirty Pieces of Silver

knew of their hatred of Jesus. He had seen the sharp confrontation with him the day before. He was, however, still unsure of how his betrayal would be received. Nervously he asked, "What are you willing to give me if I hand him over to you?" [5] He was pleased by the friendly reception of his offer. Three or four men gathered around Caiaphas and discussed the amount in question. This was the break they had been waiting for. They did not want to miss this opportunity. With some legal precedence,[6] they promised Judas thirty pieces of silver if he agreed to deliver Jesus into their hands.[7] He agreed. Perhaps he would even be accepted as a hero in their midst, someone who had helped Israel solve this troubling issue.

The money from the temple treasury was brought forward, and Judas watched carefully as one by one the coins were laid upon the scale.[8] As the clank of each coin resounded through the room, each heart was made glad; Judas' greed was fulfilled and the Jewish leaders' big break realized. The coins were handed over and Caiaphas made it clear to Judas that they could not arrest Jesus in public. The uproar it would cause would put their own positions in jeopardy, not to mention the displeasure it would bring to their Roman governor, Pilate. The arrest must be made apart from the crowd.[9] Judas agreed.

Judas left, money in hand. As he walked back to Bethany, he began to think of when and where he could betray his Master. With each step

---

5   Matthew 26:15
6   The Law of Moses states that if a servant was gored by a man's ox and killed he owed the owner of the servant thirty pieces of silver, and the ox was to be stoned; Exodus 21:32
7   Mark 14:11
8   "'They weight unto him'; or very literally, 'they placed for him (in the balance)'. Although coined shekels were in circulation, weighing appears to have been practiced, especially when considerable sums were paid out of the temple treasury" Vincent word studies on Matthew 26:15
9   Luke 22:6

he made, the coins jingled in the bag tied about his waist. As he departed the city, the temple gates were being closed as the priests began their preparations for the Passover.

With the arrival of the first three stars of Wednesday evening, the 14th of Nisan began, marking the beginning of the seven days of Unleavened Bread, highlighted by the eating of the Passover on the 15th of Nisan.

On this night Jesus lay down for the last time upon the earth he helped create. As the moon cast its soft shadows upon Bethany's landscape, Lazarus, Mary and Martha, Peter, James, and John all lay in restless sleep in anticipation of the greatest day on the Jewish calendar. On this night Judas likewise slept his last, if he slept at all, with a bag of coins for his pillow.

As darkness turned to dawn, the characters that would participate in the greatest event in man's history began to stir. Jesus had done all he could do to work God's will. Satan had done all he could do to destroy it.

The last day had arrived.

Chapter Two

Peter and John Make Ready

> *"Then came the first day of Unleavened Bread on which the Passover lamb had to be sacrificed."*
>
> Luke 22:7

With the sun rising on Thursday morning, time began to move quickly as the Passover lamb was to be sacrificed at the end of the day. There were preparations to be made. As the Apostles greeted Jesus in the Thursday morning light, he singled out Peter and John. "Go and prepare the Passover for us, that we may eat it."[1] They responded with, "Where?"[2] Because of the large numbers of pilgrims who attended the feast, excep-

---

1 Luke 22:8
2 Matthew 26:17; Mark 14:12; Luke 22:9

tions were made that did allow for eating the Passover around Mt. Olivet, including Bethany. Yet Jesus made it clear that he would be entering the city for this most important event.

With Judas listening carefully for any information about the location, the Lord was careful in his wording so as to prevent a premature arrest. "Go into Jerusalem, and after you have entered the city you will see a man carrying a pitcher of water; follow him into the house that he enters." Then he instructed the duo, "Say to the owner of the house, 'The Teacher says to you, "Where is the guest room in which I may eat the Passover with my disciples."'"

As directed, Peter, the mature fisherman, headed into the city with his youthful sidekick John. They had the task of finding this one man among the crowds that had filled the city on this great exciting feast day. Oh well, Jesus had told them that they would become fishers of men. Now they had to catch one man in a sea of humanity. But the task was not as great as it seemed as few men were encumbered with the responsibility of fetching water. This was a job almost exclusively assigned to women.[3] The man should not be hard to spot, and would no doubt be embarrassed to be found with a water jug upon his head.

As they walked through the city and their eyes searched the crowd, they soon spotted a young man carrying the pitcher of water. He was a young man they knew. They followed him into the courtyard of his spacious home. It was Mark, whose mother Mary had sent him on his

---

3   Hendriksen, p 567

embarrassing journey as she was busy with preparations.[4] They were disciples of Jesus. Peter and John asked, "Where is the guest room in which the Teacher may eat the Passover with his disciples?" They were led up an outside staircase and shown a large upper room that was apart from the main house. As they entered, they saw the couches and low tables, with cushions about, where they would recline as they ate. There was a basin of water and towels for the washing of feet. They were assured that everything was ready to be served, as Jesus had said;[5] the unleavened cakes, the bitter herbs, the dish of vinegar, the wine and needed vessels.[6] Completing the room were the festive lamps that would give light during the evening feast.

The only thing left to be provided was the sacrificial lamb. Peter and John made their way toward the temple. They waited their turn among the growing masses to claim their young lamb at the sheep market. The lamb was purchased the day before by Judas, allowing proper time for Levitical inspection to make sure it had no spot or blemish. Claiming their lamb, they walked to the temple and joined the large throng of pilgrims who were waiting for the temple gates to open.

At 2:30 in the afternoon there were three blasts of the silver trumpets as the priests marked the beginning of Passover sacrifices.[7] The temple grounds were filled with hundreds of white robed priests and Levites called into temple duty. The gates were opened and tens of thousands

---

4   This speculation is not original with me, but speculation nonetheless. I find it more than plausible. The church would later meet at Mary and John Mark's house (Acts 12:12). This house had a large upper room in which Jesus observed the Passover and where Mark followed the mob that went to arrest Jesus (Mark 14:51-52).
5   Luke 22:13
6   Broadhurst; p 48
7   Broadhurst; p 46

of men were given entrance into the temple in an orderly fashion, in three different divisions. The bleating of the young lambs filled the temple courts. It was an amazing scene.

Making their way to their altar, Peter and John were joined by one of the officiating priests, his white robe already blood splattered. With John holding the lamb upon the altar, Peter skillfully inserted a knife into the lamb's neck and quietly and painlessly the animal bled out.[8] The priest collected some of the blood in a bowl and passed it to others until it made its way inside the temple proper where the blood was slung from the bowl across the base of the great altar, the spiritual door of Israel. Meanwhile the priest removed the parts of the lamb that were to be burned upon the altar. Then the sacrifice was laid on staves and carried out on the shoulders of Peter and John.

As they made their way out of the temple with the sacrifice, they joined in the antiphonal singing of the Hallel, the songs of Psalms 113-118. The sound of singing filled the temple air, as did the smell of blood.

Arriving back at the upper room, they began to roast the lamb. The Passover meal was almost ready.

---

[8] There were brief periods in Israel's history where the priests performed the sacrifices, but during Jesus' day, and through most of history, the laymen sacrificed the lambs, and the priests were in charge of the blood; Broadhurst p 46

Chapter Three

The Upper Room

> *"And when the hour had come, He reclined at the table, and the apostles with him."*
>
> Luke 22:14

As the sun set over Zion's hill, eleven sets of sandals journeyed down Olivet's mount. With Peter and John waiting, Jesus and the other apostles made their way toward the upper chamber of the guest room. It had been a solemn journey for the Lord. With each step he drew nearer Golgotha's hill. Each minute the crack of the scourger's whip rang louder in his ears. Every moment the words of Isaiah were further fulfilled:

"He was despised and forsaken of men,

A man of sorrows and acquainted with grief.

And like one from whom men hide their face

He was despised, and we did not esteem Him.

Surely our griefs He Himself bore,

And our sorrows He carried;

Yet we ourselves esteemed Him stricken,

Smitten of God, and afflicted."[1]

With the last light disappearing over the city, Jesus entered with little notice. After arriving at the home of Mark's parents, there was a short period of fellowship in the courtyard as the ingredients of the supper were carried into the upper room and the lamb completed the roasting. It was now officially Friday night, the 15th of Nisan.[2] The Passover had arrived.[3] It was Jesus' desire that this Passover be a private meal with only his Ttwelve.[4] The women, and other family members, would gather around other tables. The upper room would give him the privacy he desired. While it was a festive time in the city, the Lord's face and mood cast a

---

1   Isaiah 53:3-4
2   This was Thursday night by our modern calendars. The Jewish day started at sundown rather than at midnight.
3   For well over a hundred years some have argued that the meal Jesus ate was not the Passover, but a separate dinner eaten on Wednesday evening instead of Thursday. This argument centers around some of John's comments and the desire to have Jesus crucified on Thursday at the same time the Lambs were being sacrificed in the temple. But Jesus uses the Greek word "pascha" several times in the text, which was the specific term for the sacrificed lamb of the Passover. This and the Synoptic Gospels' specific language make it clear that Jesus ate the sacrificed, roasted Passover lamb in the upper room on the 15th of Nisan. For a greater explanation see Edersheim, *The Life and Times of Jesus the Messiah*, Book 5, chapter 10, Page 554.
4   Matthew 26:20, Mark 14:17,20; While originally the Passover was to be eaten in groups of ten, by Jesus' day it had changed to groups of up to twenty. "Because of the great multitude of people involved, some of the original laws about Passover had to be altered." Broadhurst, p 47

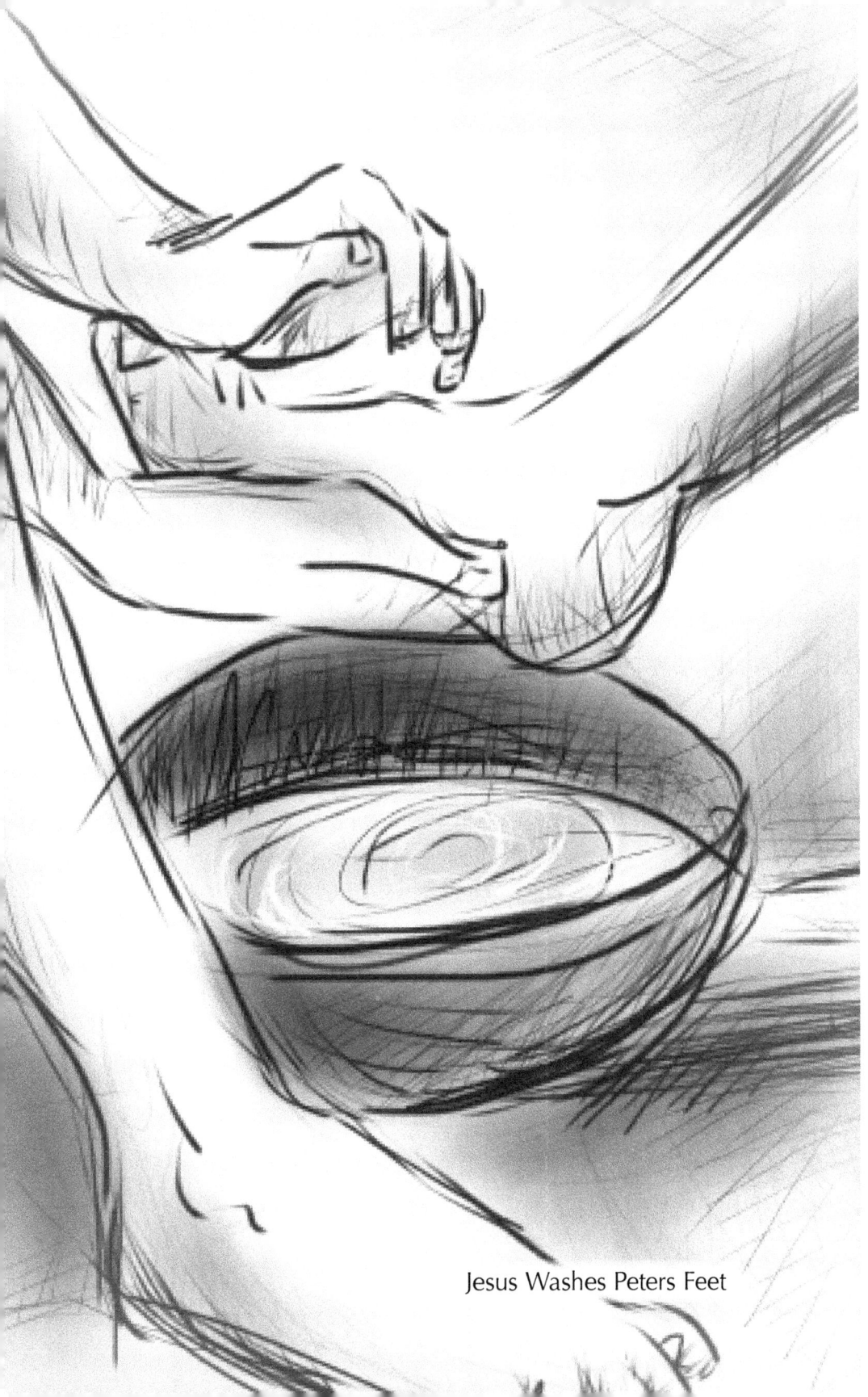
Jesus Washes Peters Feet

quiet and solemn net over the men gathered around the roasting lamb. When everything was ready, and at the Lord's motion, the men walked up the staircase into the upper room, with Jesus following.

As each man entered the room, he removed his sandals and placed them on mats around the wall. The traditional table was kidney-shaped to allow seating all around, with an open area for servants to place the food in front of the host, who sat in the middle of the table with the guests on either side.[5] Jesus entered the room and reclined at the head of the table, as he was the host. As he was taking his seat, he noticed some shuffling among his men, as each tried to outdo the other to get a place as close to the Lord as they could. In the haste to gain a more prominent position around the table, they failed to take the time to wash their feet, now dusty from the walk into the city. Judas procured the prominent place to the Lord's left.[6] To his right side was John, the youngest and one known to hold a special place in Jesus' heart.[7] The other places were still up for grabs. On such an important occasion, each man quietly fought for a place close to the Lord. Peter would have none of this, and went to the end of the table, on John's side, and reclined.

In this shuffling about to get a desired spot, the Apostles began to argue with each other as to whom Jesus regarded as the greatest among them.[8] In the midst of this Jesus quietly rose, hardly noticed by the men preoccupied in quiet debate, and walked over to the basin of water and

---

5   Edersheim; *The Life and Times of Jesus the Messiah,* Chapter X, p 560; he describes the table as almost "horseshoe shaped." This allowed for food to be brought in and placed before the host, and by tradition to allow the dishes to be removed after the feast, while other activities took place.
6   John 13:26; Edersheim, Chapter X, pg. 560
7   John 13:23
8   Luke 22:24; see also Farrar; p 556

The Upper Room

towels. He removed his robe. As he did so, first one head turned to look, and then another, and another, until at last all the debate was silenced as twelve sets of eyes became fixed on Jesus in a stare of quiet curiosity. Bare-chested, Jesus next removed his tunic.[9] Now in only his loincloth he took the common linen towel used for this purpose and wrapped it about his waist, picked up the basin of water, and turned back toward his men. With quick looks of bewilderment at one another, they could not imagine what he was doing.

Jesus first came to Peter, who was reclined at the end of the table. He knelt at Peter's feet and placed the water basin on the floor. Realizing what Jesus was about to do, Peter quickly drew his feet back and sat up abruptly, "Lord, are you going to wash my feet?" he asked in bewildered tones. The other men looked on in shock seeing the Master now dressed as a common slave and doing a slave's work.

"What I do now," Jesus said to Peter, "You may not understand, but you will understand later."

But Peter's low self-esteem was having none of it. "No Lord!" he objected. "You will never wash my feet; never!" The very idea was anathema to Peter who had fallen at Jesus' feet early on and proclaimed, "Go away from me Lord, for I am a sinful man."[10] Now Jesus was kneeling at his feet, wanting to wash them! Peter was not about to let that happen.

But Jesus was tenderly insistent. He looked into Peter's dark, confused eyes and explained softly, "If I do not wash you, you have no part of me."

---

9   John 13:4; "laid aside his garments" was plural indicating both his outer robe and his tunic. The plural was also used when the Roman soldiers cast lots for his "garments" in John 19:23-24.
10   Luke 5:8

Peter gazed back into the Lord's face for a moment and allowed his words to sink deep into his heart. Slowly he slid his feet out to the Master's basin. "Then Lord, wash not only my feet," his said, "but my head and my hands."

Jesus washed Peter's feet.

"There," he said to Peter as he finished, "you are clean now." Then gazing over Peter's shoulder Jesus remarked, "You are clean, but not all of you are clean."

Then he moved on to Andrew and James and Thomas; next to John, and then to Judas Iscariot. Yes, Jesus poured water over the feet of Judas and gently wiped them clean, drying them with the towel about his waist. As a true servant, he had no choice about whose feet he washed.

Completing his task and having washed all twelve, he retrieved his tunic and robe and took his place back at the table. "Do you know what I have done to you?" he asked his men. There was dead silence. "You call me 'Teacher' and 'Lord' and you were right, for so I am. But I have given you an example of how you are to wash each other's feet; to humble yourselves to one another, as I humble myself to the one that sent me. You will be blessed if you do this. But I do not speak of all of you for the Scripture will be fulfilled, 'He who eats my bread has lifted up his heel against me.'"[11]

Never again will these men seek the best seats around the table or seek out some high position in the kingdom of God.

11   John 13: 5-20

"For You Are Clean, But Not All Of You" For He Knew The One Who Was Betraying Him.

Chapter Four

Judas and the Sop

> *"When Jesus had said this, He became troubled in spirit, and testified and said, 'Truly, truly, I say to you, that one of you will betray me.'"*
>
> John 13:21

Now as they all reclined around the table, Jesus began by saying, "I have earnestly desired to eat this Passover with you before I suffer; for I say to you, I shall never again eat it, until it is fulfilled in the kingdom of God."[1] God's plan for saving man was about to reach its grand climax. This was truly the last Passover. What this memorial meal was about to become, would next be eaten in the kingdom of God.

---

1   Luke 22:14-16; "In the original institution, the Passover was to be eaten standing (Exod. 12:11). After the Capitivity [in Babylon and the return,] the custom was changed, and the guests reclined." Vincent on John 13:25

The supper began in the traditional way with the host offering a cup of blessing upon the Passover. By tradition, the host was to remind his group of what God did for Israel when he brought them out of Egyptian bondage.[2] On this occasion Jesus' words did not follow that tradition. "Take this and share it among yourselves," he said as he offered the first cup. "For I say to you, that I will not drink of this fruit of the vine in the future, until I drink it with you in a new manner, in my Father's kingdom."[3]

With the supper now begun, Jesus, as host, took a piece of the lamb, wrapped it in the unleavened bread and dipped it into the "sop," that mixture of bitter herbs, vinegar, and salt, and began to pass it around to each man about the table. As he did so, the anger built within his human spirit toward the one who would betray him.[4] This greedy thief had the nerve to partake of this sacred meal, the gall to claim the seat closest to him, all the while looking for a chance to betray. The Lord could tolerate such hypocrisy no longer, nor share this sacred time with such a man. Jesus was through with Judas.

A stern voice broke the silence of this Passover meal. "Truly, truly I say to you, one of you will betray me! One of you who is eating with me!"[5] The disciples froze. They began to look at one another, then to Jesus. Now each moment of distrust, every memory of their own self doubt, and each day of failing faith flashed through their minds. Every heart beating around that table beat faster. "Lord is it I?" "Surely not I!" each man spoke

---

2 There may have been as many as four ceremonial cups of wine drunk at the Passover during Jesus' day. We are unsure, but in the third century we read of four cups being used. Jesus at least used three, and perhaps four. The Jews today continue to use four cups during their Passover observance. See Broadhurst; p 49
3 See Luke 22:14-18
4 John 13:21a
5 John 13:21b; Mark 14:18

Road To The Upper Room

to the Lord. "Surely not I," each said to assure the brother next to him.

As the proclamations echoed around the room, Peter, from his position at the end of the horseshoe-shaped table, got John's attention as he reclined next to Jesus. Peter was anxious to find out who this traitor was so that he could perhaps deal with him in his own way. Half gesturing and half moving his lips, he communicated to John, "Get him to tell you who it is he is speaking of." John needed little encouragement, and leaned in close, his cheek near to Jesus' ear, "Lord, who is it?" he asked in whispered tones.

Jesus reached for another piece of unleavened bread, wrapped a bit of roasted lamb in it, and, turning his face toward John said softly, "It is the one for whom I shall dip the morsel and give it to him."

Then dipping it into the sop, Jesus turned and handed it to Judas Iscariot. As Judas took it their eyes met. "Surely it is not I, Rabbi?" Judas asked.[6] "Yes, Judas, by your own admission, it is you!" Jesus replied. He knew then that Jesus knew. With a heart as hardened as the Pharaoh whose escape they celebrated, Judas swallowed the morsel as a small smile creased his lips. It was the smirk of Satan.

"What you are about to do, do it now!" Jesus commanded. Judas immediately rose, left the room, and disappeared into the night. With all the stunning events taking place in the upper room the other men could scarcely put it all together. Perhaps Judas was going out to run other errands for the Lord, or maybe Jesus had asked him to go make a donation

---

6   Matthew 26:25

Judas and the Sop

for the poor in the temple, which was open during the Passover.[7] But as others were distracted by Judas' departure, John turned and looked at Peter and nodded. In Gethsemane their suspicions would be confirmed.

In the darkness of the night, Judas paused, his mind racing and his pulse pounding, as he gathered his thoughts. Once again he made his way past the shops and bakeries, around one corner and then another, upon the stone paved streets and beneath the rock archways until he found himself once again standing in front of the house of the high priest. It was time to earn his silver.

In the upper room, the Passover meal was about to take on a new meaning.

---

7   Hendriksen points out that in this large city on such an important occasion that there would be certain places where needed items could still be purchased. The Passover was an all night celebration. The Temple and its treasury would be open and donations could be made all during the night; Hendriksen, commentary on John 13:29

Chapter Five

The Bread and the Cup

"Do this in remembrance of me."

Luke 22:19

With the departure of Judas from the upper room, Jesus knew that the hourglass had been turned. The betrayer was about his business, so now the betrayed must be about his. Jesus took one of the "loaves," the flat unleavened bread of the Passover, the bread first eaten in the bondage of Egypt, and blessed it with a prayer.

Heretofore the bread was used to eat with the lamb, to dip in the bitter herbs; but no longer. Heretofore the loaf was a symbol of that happy day of deliverance from Pharaoh's chains, but no more. Heretofore the unleavened bread was the bread of haste, but not now.

Breaking the bread and passing one part to his right, the other to his left, he said, "Take, eat, this is my body which is given for you. Do this in remembrance of me."[1]

Silently they partook; silently they considered his words.

Next Jesus took the cup and blessed it too. The cup of wine had been added by tradition and had become an important part of the Passover celebration.

Heretofore the wine was a symbol of joy and happiness, but no longer. Heretofore the fruit of the vine was used as a moment of blessing, but no more. Heretofore the cup was the cup of Israel, a symbol of its greatness; but not now.

Taking the cup, he presented it to his Apostles, saying, "This cup is poured out for you, it is the new covenant in my blood. It will be poured out for many for the forgiveness of sins. I say now to you that I will not drink of this fruit of the vine from now on until that day when I drink it new with you in my Father's kingdom. Do this, as often as you drink it, in remembrance of me."[2]

With the institution of this new memorial meal, Jesus told them, "My little children, I am with you a little while longer. You will seek me; as I told the Jews, now I also say to you, where I am going, you cannot come." Knowing that he would soon be taken away from them he gave them this important commandment; "Love one another, even as I have loved you."[3]

1   Luke 22:19; 1 Corinthians 11:23-24
2   Matthew 26:27-29; 1 Corinthians 11:25
3   John 13:33-35

The Bread and the Cup

Jesus praised his eleven men; "You are those who have stood by me in my trials; My Father has granted me a kingdom, and I grant you that you may eat and drink at my table, and you will sit on thrones judging the twelve tribes of Israel."[4]

Fully aware that his hour had come, that soon he would be taken from them, knowing that even this night they would have to contend with the forces of evil alone, he turned to Peter and said, "Simon, Simon, behold, Satan is anxious to separate you from me, like the chaff was separated from the wheat," Satan had conquered the weakest of the twelve, now he sought the strongest. "I am praying for you," Jesus said, "that your faith will not fail and that as you learn to deal with this evil, you will turn and strengthen your brothers."[5]

Peter responded, "Oh no Lord! I am ready to go to prison with you, or even to death!"

"Oh no Peter," Jesus replied, "Before the rooster crows two times, you will deny me three times."[6]

Before Peter could rebut, Jesus asked his men, "When I sent you out before, without a money belt, or a bag, or sandals, did you lack anything during your mission?"

They all responded, "No, nothing."

---

4   Luke 22:28-30
5   Luke 22:31-32; my paraphrase. The word "sift" in the text was used only here in the N.T.; it refers to the separating of the chaff from the wheat. The whole context of Luke 22:28-38 was dealing with Jesus' concern for the Apostles after he was arrested and separated from them. They have looked to him for everything up to now. But soon they would have to fend for themselves.
6   Mark 14:30; Luke 22:33,34; John 13:37-38;

Knowing that he would not be with them during their next mission, he encouraged them, "But now take a money belt, take a bag," and knowing of the personal dangers they would encounter, "if you don't have a sword: get one!"

They said, "Lord, look, here are two swords." And he said to them, "It is enough."[7]

---

[7] Luke 22:38

Chapter Six
"Let Not Your Heart Be Troubled"

> "Do not let your heart be troubled; believe in God, believe also in Me."
>
> John 14:1

It had been an emotionally draining night for the Apostles. The humbling lesson of Jesus washing their feet, his talk of a betrayer, the symbolic meaning of his death he had given to the unleavened bread and wine, had engulfed the room in a cloud of sorrow. The somber tone of the Lord and the serious content of his statements, combined with the importance of this great feast, had put a great weight upon their hearts.

As they remained reclined around the Passover table, Jesus felt the need to encourage his men. Judas had gone out into the night. Hungry stomachs had given way to troubled hearts. As flickering lamps cast woeful shadows of each figure along the walls of the upper room, and with John resting on his shoulder, Jesus spoke.

"Let not your hearts be troubled," he said in uplifting and almost cheerful tones. "You believe in God, believe also in me. In my Father's house are many dwelling places; if it were not so, I would have told you; for I go to prepare a place for you. If I go and prepare a place for you, I will come again and receive you to myself, that where I am, there you may be also. And you know the way where I am going."[1]

Thomas spoke up, his comment reflecting the sentiments of them all; "Lord, we do not know where you are going, how do we know the way?"

"I am the way; and the truth, and the life; no one comes to the Father but through me."[2]

Jesus went on to explain that while he must leave them, they would not be left alone. "I will ask the Father, and He will give you another Helper, that he may be with you forever; that Helper is the Spirit of truth."

Jesus assured them that he would not leave them as "orphans."[3]

"The Holy Spirit, whom the Father will send in My name, He will teach you all things, and bring to your remembrance all that I said to you...Peace I leave with you, my peace I give to you... Do not let your heart be troubled."[4]

A short distance away Judas was busy gathering his mob.[5] Divinely

1 John 14:1-4
2 John 14: 5-6
3 John 14:16-18
4 John 14:26-27
5 John 18:3

aware of this, Jesus brought to a conclusion the events in the upper room. "I will not speak much more with you, for the ruler of the world is coming."

"Get up, let us go from here."[6]

It was traditional for the Passover to end in a song. As they stood, they sang.

---

6   John 14:31; The great message of the vine and the branches of John 15, the tender words to his disciples preparing them for his death in John 16, and the powerful prayer to his Father in John 17, all took place somewhere between or along the path from the upper room, across the Kidron valley, and up into the Garden of Gethsemane. Knowing that Judas would be coming to the upper room first, Jesus knew he could not tarry there and complete his words. Also, he greatly longed for the solitude of Gethsemane's shadows.

Chapter Seven
Out to Gethsemene

"After singing a hymn, they went out to the Mount of Olives."
Matthew 26:30

Israel did not have a national anthem as such, but it did have its great "Hallel." This was a song composed from the psalms of David, using Psalm 113 through Psalm 118. These were psalms of praise, thanksgiving, and trust. The "song" began with:

"Praise the Lord! Praise, O servants of the LORD,
"Praise the name of the LORD."

And concluded with;

"Give thanks to the LORD, for He is good;

For His lovingkindness is everlasting."

It was sung on many special occasions and was known by heart by most of the adult population. It was sung by the congregation in the temple during the Feast of Dedication. It was sung by the priests as they sacrificed the lambs during the Passover. It was also sung, in parts generally, during the Passover, as a part of the various cups of blessing that were offered during this great meal. The final part was traditionally sung to conclude the feast.[1]

In the final part the words were reflective of the Messiah as he concluded his supper:

"The stone which the builders rejected

Has become the chief corner stone."[2]

Jesus and his men rose from the table to sing - not as a choir of great operatic quality, but as a solemn dirge of men's deep voices. The Lord's life was announced with the call of angels across shepherds' fields, and now concluded with twelve men's hoarse voices in weary song. Ending the song they went out.

After singing this great Psalm, they left the upper room;

The Lord teaching and praying along they way.

After singing this sacred hymn, they went out;

Down the steps, past Siloam's pool, and over Kidron's creek.

---

1   Farrar, p 563, also Broadhurst, p 50; Hendriksen's commentary on Matthew 26:30; Jews today still sing the Hallel, and it is still sung to conclude the Passover.
2   Psalm 118:22

The Betrayer's Kiss

Road To The Upper Room

    They went out; out to the Mount of Olives as was his custom;[3]

        Into the shadows of Gethsemane, where in sorrow they soon slept.[4]

    And as they slept he prayed;

    Prayed as sweat like drops of blood dripped from his skin.[5]

    Submitting to the will of his Father, and awaiting the betrayer's kiss.

---

[3]   Luke 22:39
[4]   Luke 22:45
[5]   Luke 22:44

Epilogue

> *"But standing by the cross of Jesus were His mother, and His mother's sister, Mary the wife of Clopas, and Mary Magdalene. When Jesus then saw His mother and the disciple whmo He loved standing nearby, He said to His mother, 'Woman, behold, your son!'"*
>
> John 19:25, 26

Each of us now stands in the darkness, on Golgotha's hill, gazing upon the shadowy figure of a dead man hanging on a tree. Now we know his story. We know how through the weakness of men, and the greatness of sin, he came to be here.

Peer through the darkness and see the open wound in his side. See the lifeless hands whose flesh has been torn by rusty Roman nails. See the crown of thorns that sits upon his blood-matted hair. Step forward. Walk up to the base of the cross and look down at the pool of blood staining God's earth. Look up into the face of the Savior and realize that he died an innocent man. All he did was to teach great lessons, heal all manner of sickness, raise the dead, care for his mother, help the helpless, and pray to his father. He was totally innocent. But look upon him, remember his story, and realize he was there because he and his Father love you.

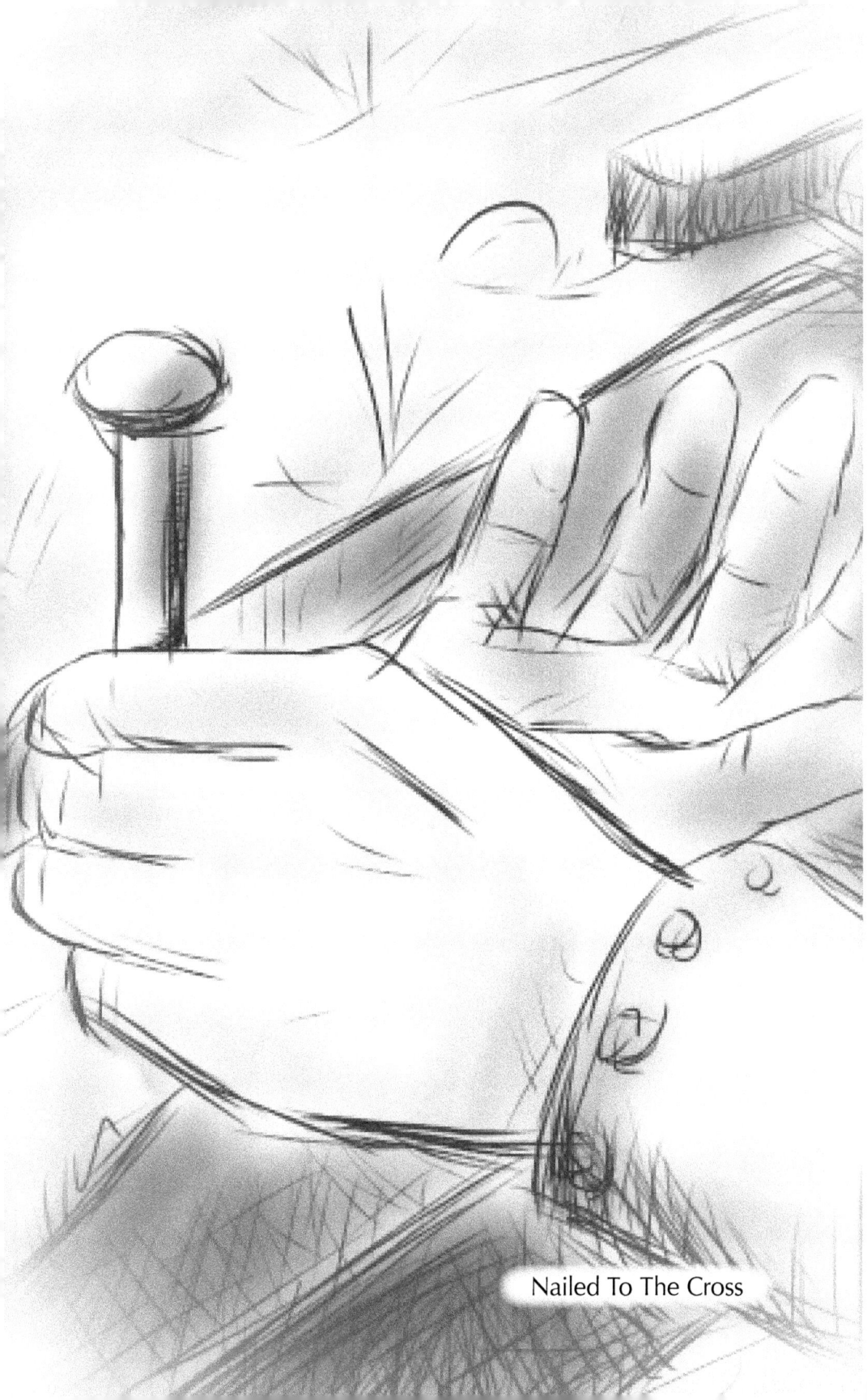
Nailed To The Cross

Behold Him!

Behold Him in the manger,
 the earthly form of God's love.
Listen as the host of angels
 sing to the shepherds from above.

Behold Him on the mountainside
 as he teaches the multitudes.
Join Him as He feeds them all
 with only two fish for food.

Behold Him as he heals the sick;
 the blind, the leper, the lame.
Walk with Him into Jerusalem
 as the crowds shout out His name.

Behold Him in Gethsemane
 as He prepares to die.
Watch Him before Pilate
 as the mob cries, "Crucify!"

Behold Him on the cross
 in a darkened noonday sky.
Stand silent as the stone rolls back
 and angels proclaim "He's alive!"

Behold Him. Oh, behold Him!
 His hands and feet nail-scarred,
Behold Him. Oh, behold Him!
 Will you now follow His star?

-Dennis Doughty

Jesus' Hands

The Lessons

Section Four

Lesson One
The Last Months

Review Section 1 of the book – "The Last Months"
Read John 10:22-42

What Did You Learn?

Discussion Points:

1. What new things did you learn about Jesus in this section? How did the narrative make the story come alive?
2. What did you learn about the customs and lifestyle of Jesus' day from this section?
3. What did you learn from the Scriptures in this section that you had not known before? Or thought about before?

Lesson Two
The Last Week

Review Section 2 – "The Last Week"

Read John 12:9-19

What Did You Learn?

Discussion Points:

1. What new things did you learn about Jesus in this section? How did the narrative make the story come alive?

2. What did you learn about the customs and lifestyle of Jesus' day from this section?

3. What did you learn from the Scriptures in this section that you had not known before? Or thought about before?

Lesson Three
The Last Day

Review Section 3 – "The Last Day"

Read John 13:1-20

What Did You Learn?

Discussion points:

1. What new things did you learn about Jesus in this section? How did the narrative make the story come alive?

2. What did you learn about the customs and lifestyle of Jesus' day from this section?

3. What did you learn from the Scriptures in this section that you had not known before? Or thought about before?

Lesson Four
Christ's Greatest Miracle

Read Section 1, Chapters 4-7

Read John 11:1-57

The Facts:

Jesus did many wonderful miracles while he was in the flesh. So many that "if every one of them were written down, I suppose that even the whole world would not have room for the books that would be written (John 21:25). Which miracle was his greatest? We could try to rank them in some order;

- Fishing Tips: At least twice Jesus gave advice about where to let down the nets, and each time a great catch was the result (Luke 5:4-6; John 21:4-6). While many fishermen today might love to have this kind of knowledge, we would probably not give these miracles a very high rating on our scale.

- Food Production: On two occasions Jesus turned a few loaves of bread and a few fish into a large meal feeding first five thousand and then four thousand (Matthew 14:13-21; 15:32-38). A great feat, but not many of us would rate it as his greatest.

- Medical Cures: Jesus cured everything from the high fever that Peter's mother-in-law had (Luke 4:38-39) to a lady (Mary Magdalene) who kept losing blood (Mark 5:25-34); and various other diseases (Luke 4:40). While impressive, we today see the modern miracles done by our doctors, medicines, and treatments which might take away the impact of such actions in Christ's day. We certainly would rate these high on the scale, but we are still not quite at the top.

- Control over Nature: Jesus' power over the laws of nature certainly ranks high on the list of Jesus' most impressive miracles. His ability to walk on the water and to command the wind to "Be still," astonished and even frightened his own Apostles (Mark 4:35-41; 6:45-52). Now we are surely getting closer to his greatest miracle!

- Raising the Dead: On three occasions Jesus raised the dead. Even today this stands alone as the greatest miracle of all; to restore life to the dead. The physician Luke writes of Jesus raising the widow's son, and restoring life to the young twelve-year-old daughter of Jarius (Luke 7:11- 15; 8:40-56). Both had been dead for a very short time, just a few hours at most, and the incidents occurred in the region of Galilee. There were few witnesses, and Jesus even asked that the events be kept secret. The third occasion was the raising of Lazarus. When we examine the circumstances, the witnesses, and the influence of this event, we may well conclude that this was Jesus' greatest miracle!

The Points:

The Humanity of Christ: In the story of the death of Lazarus and the events that lead up to him being raised, we see a great deal of emotion. We can expect such emotion where the death of a loved one is involved. Yet the emotion we see in Christ is perhaps a little unexpected. He is the Son of God, and he knows he is going to raise his friend from the dead. So why the tears? Why is his spirit stirred within him as he walks to the tomb? (John 11:35-38) The only answer is that in this very emotional setting, Jesus' humanity could not be suppressed.

We fail to grasp just how much of a flesh and blood man Jesus was. The Word became "flesh" (John 1:14), and in this fleshly form he worked, loved his mother, got tired and hungry, laughed and frowned, and bled and died as any man. The despair he heard in Martha's voice, the tears he saw in Mary's eyes, and the grief he felt from the crowd produced strong emotions in this man.

We can rejoice in his tears. We must celebrate the fact that God became a man. Now we have a High Priest sitting in Heaven that can identify with our grief. "For since he himself was tempted in that which he suffered, he is able to come to the aid of those who are tempted" (Hebrews 2:18).

The Power of Christ: It is on this occasion that Jesus links our own deaths to his power to raise us from the dead. We are Lazarus. We all will die and be placed in our own tombs. To us he proclaims, "I am the resurrection and the life; he who believes in Me will live even if he dies, and everyone who lives and believes in Me will never die. Do you believe this?" (John 11:25-26) Well, do YOU believe this?

When Jesus called out, "Lazarus come forth" he was showing us his power. He was in effect telling us that some day he will call out our names. The gates of Paradise will swing out and we will all come forth! Do you believe this? This great event gives us tremendous faith in Christ having the power to do what he said he would do. The raising of Lazarus was so dramatic and convincing that his enemies could not disprove what happened. Lazarus had become a walking billboard of Jesus' power. Their response serves to strengthen our faith in this story. If they could have disproved what happened, they would have. In the end their only solution was to plan the deaths of both men (John 11:53; 12:10).

The Influence of Christ: This miracle was done before a great crowd of influential Jews from the Jerusalem area. They saw Lazarus come out of the tomb. This event was polarizing. John 11:45-46 tells us of the response to this great miracle. "Many" believed in him. "Some" went high-tailing it to the Pharisees and told what happened.

Jesus has always been a polarizing figure. He himself said, "He who is not with me, is against me, and he who does not gather with me scatters" (Matthew 12:30). The events of the raising of Lazarus had catapulted the work of Jesus into the stratosphere! This is clearly seen when he at last enters the city of Jerusalem a few weeks later during the week of the Passover. They rushed out of the city to meet him, so much so that the Pharisees sadly admit to each other that "the world has gone after him" (John 12:17-19).

What Do You Think?

1. Would you agree or disagree that the raising of Lazarus was Jesus' greatest miracle? How would you rate his miracles?
2. When Jesus returned to Bethany he was going into a dangerous situation. Have you ever thought of that before? Have you ever gone into a situation which you knew beforehand was going to be a dangerous one? What does this teach us about Christ?
3. In chapter six of the narrative, the scene of the raising of Lazarus is described. What about that scene does the narrative reveal to you that you had not thought of before? What impressed you about the raising of Lazarus?

Lesson Five
The Fruitless Fig Tree
Read the Narrative, Section 2, Chapters 7-8
Read: Matthew 21:18-22; Mark 11:12-14, 20-26

The Facts:

- The fig tree is native to the area. It can grow to a height of about fifteen feet. The fruit is unique in that the bloom closes instead of opens. As the leaves grow about it, the bloom develops into its fruit, therefore a tree whose leaves are fully developed is a sign that it is ready to be harvested. In warm climates it would yield two crops, one from the old wood in the spring, and one from the new spring sprouts about August.[1]

- The fig tree in Israel was more than just a plant; it was symbolic of their nation. The fig tree and its fruit is mentioned more than sixty times in the Bible, and most of the time is used in a symbolic way. Compare the basket of the good and bad figs God showed to Jeremiah (Jeremiah 24:1-7).

- When Jesus cursed the fig tree, it was not the first time God had destroyed this tree. David wrote that when God sent the plagues against Egypt that "He struck down their vines also and their fig trees" (Psalm 105:33).

- The fig tree was present in the Garden of Eden and was put to good use by Adam and Eve. How did they use it? See Genesis 3:7.

[1] International Standard Bible Encyclopedia; Eerdmans Publishers, Grand Rapids Mich.;1956 edition

The Points:

Importance of the Event: In an interesting kind of way the cursing of the fig tree is one of the more significant and symbolic events of the final few days of our Lord. Most commentators come to this miracle and just scratch their heads. It seems so "out of character for Jesus to use his powers in a negative way" they say. He is always healing, not destroying. But this event:

1. Helps establish the chronology for the days of Monday and Tuesday; therefore it is an important "marker" in having a better understanding of these days.
2. Symbolizes the lack of spiritual service Israel gave to God and the rejection of his Son. The fruit of Israel was to produce a savior, from whom "all the nations of the earth would be blessed" (Genesis 12:3). In rejecting that savior, rejecting "the chief corner stone," it had become unfruitful (Matthew 21:42-43).
3. To those that see this miracle as "out of character" for Christ, they only need read 2 Thessalonians 1:7-8 as Jesus returns from heaven "with his mighty angels in flaming fire dealing out retribution to those who do not know God and to those who do not obey the gospel of our Lord Jesus Christ."

The Need to Produce Fruit: Jesus expects our Christian life not to be about the leaves, but the fruit. Sadly much Christian service today is about appearances. That was the problem with the Pharisees as they did "all their deeds to be noticed by men; for they broaden their phylacteries and lengthen the tassels of their garments" (Matthew 23:5).

Christian living is all about producing fruit. Jesus told the parable of the vineyard keeper who begged to keep a fig tree which had been unproductive for three years. "If it bears fruit next year, fine! If not, cut it down" (Luke 13:6-9). God is a gracious and patient vineyard keeper; he gives us time to grow and mature, but at some point in our lives he expects us to begin using our talents, time and skills in serving him (John 15:1-8). In cursing the fig tree Jesus shows his disdain for fruitlessness!

The Faith to Move Mountains: Besides the point Jesus made in cursing the tree, he also made a great point to his disciples about the power of the prayer of faith. While they were surprised at the power of his words against a small tree, Jesus told them that the prayer of faith could toss the mountain they were standing on into the Dead Sea below them. Faith and prayer together are a powerful combination.

I heard a story long ago about a woman who heard her preacher proclaim in his sermon that "faith can move mountains." Afterwards she questioned him about that promise. Her preacher assured her that Jesus' words were correct. "Good she said, because I have a large garbage hill behind my house I want to have moved!" She went home that night and prayed and prayed. The next morning she got up and went to her kitchen window and saw that the garbage hill was still there. "Hum!" she said, "I knew it wouldn't work!"

No, prayer without faith will not work. But together they are the mightiest weapons in the world!

What Do You Think?

1. Why do you think Jesus cursed the fig tree? Could it have been out of anger or frustration? Perhaps it was just a symbolic act, but are symbolic acts common in Scriptures? Are symbolic acts important? Name other symbolic acts in Scripture.

2. What is the fruit that you are producing for the Lord at this time in your life? Is worship a fruit? Are doing good deeds a fruit? What did John the Baptist mean when he said: "bear fruit in keeping with repentance" (Luke 3:8)?

3. What is the greatest thing you have seen prayer do? How do we increase our faith in prayer? On a scale of 1-10 how would you rate your prayer life?

Lesson Six
"A Pound of Perfume"
Read Narrative Section 2, Chapter 4
Read John 12:1-11; Matthew 26:6-13; Mark 14:1-5

The Facts:

Women have always loved their perfume. Almost every woman's dresser is stocked with several fragrances. In Jesus' day perfume was quite a luxury. But for those who could afford it, it was very important, as daily bathing was not possible. Perfume, which was mostly in an oil form, was used in burial as well. To mask the odor of death, the body would be anointed with oil.

- **Nard or Spikenard** is a flowering plant that grows in the Himalayan Mountains of India. The oil comes from the roots of the plant. It has been used in the past as an herbal medicine. It is a very fragrant perfume and still in use today, especially in expensive shampoo.
- **Illustration:** In the 1920's outside of Paris, France, there was a perfumer named Ernest Beaux (Boz). A fashion designer came to him in 1922 and wanted to offer her clients her own distinct perfume. She asked Beaux to help and he made up five samples. She picked the sample that was labled "No. 5". Her name was Coco Chanel and her perfume, which she decided to call "Chanel No. 5" has become the biggest selling perfume of all time. Ten million bottles sell a year. A 3 ounce bottle today sells for around

$115; that would be $460 for a 12-ounce Roman pound. The nard in Jesus' day cost about $18,000 a pound in today's money (a year's salary). No wonder it generated such a response from Judas' greedy little heart!

- **Mary's motive:** It was a spontaneous act of pure adoration, devotion, gratitude, and worship of Jesus. He had given back to her the brother she lost in death. Everything going on in the room was totally blocked out by Mary. Her focus was totally on the Lord and in showing him how much she appreciated what he had done for her and her family.
- **Jesus' Defense of Mary:** "Let her alone." He pointed out that this act was to prepare him for his burial. Whether she intended it or not, Jesus saw this as death's anointing oil. She would later go to the grave that Sunday morning to complete her anointing.
- **Judas' Greed:** It is revealed to us that Judas was a thief and had been stealing from the Lord's treasury. He surely felt the Lord gaze into his heart and feared being found out. In this act he allowed Satan to enter his heart. His betrayal will be studied in the next lesson. Let us not let his treacherous deed mar this beautiful story.

The Points:

Let us be grateful and thankful disciples. How do you show your gratitude to Jesus for what he has done for you? Jesus is aware of an appreciative spirit; remember him asking "Were not ten healed, where are the nine?"

Does your worship ever become "spontaneous?" Do you find yourself touched by a song in a way that was totally unplanned? Lord's Supper? A teaching? Do you really worship "in the spirit" (John 4:24). Do you find yourself only going through the motions (1 Corinthians 14:15)?

What do you "lavish" upon the Lord? Do we give the scraps or the first fruits? Are we cheerful givers (2 Corinthians 9:7)? Do we first give of ourselves to the Lord (2 Corinthians 8:5)? Is our giving to the Lord "A bountiful gift and not affected by covetousness" (2 Corinthians 9:5).

What have you done, or will do for the Lord that will be remembered? "What this woman has done will also be spoken of in memory of her." We are remembering today, two thousand years later, this great act of devotion of Mary. It was a timeless act, a "beautiful work." What will you be remembered for by children, grandchildren, friends, church, community? What deed done? What gift given? What soul won?

Our Fragrant Aroma: This perfume had a wonderful, comforting, sweet smell, and "the house was filled with the fragrance of the perfume" (John 12:3). Some of the incense burned in the temple was from this spikenard. Our deeds are our fragrant aroma, our sweet incense that drifts heavenward.

"I am amply supplied, having received from Epaphroditus what you have sent, a fragrant aroma, an acceptable sacrifice, well-pleasing unto God" (Philippians 4:18).

What Do You Think?

1. When the group of ladies walked toward Jesus' tomb early that Sunday morning, Mary, the sister of Lazarus, was with them. There had not been time to properly prepare the Lord's body, to anoint it with the oils which were the custom of the day. As she walked toward the tomb in the morning light, do you think she thought of Jesus' words, "She has anointed me for my burial."?
2. In what ways do you see your own worship as becoming routine and unemotional?
3. When and in what ways can we give something to the Lord that is of great value? Do we ever do so?

Lesson Seven
"Judas: The Betrayer"
Read Section 3, Chapter 1
Read Luke 22:1-6; Matthew 26:14-16

The Facts:

Judas betrayed his Master. His actions have made him one of the most despised men in history. His name is forever synonymous with the term: Betrayer. No mother would dare give their baby boy this name. No sin is so despised as betrayal. Is it possible to understand his actions? Let us look at the man:

- Judean. The term "Iscariot" meant "man of Kerioth" which was a small village in Judea. This meant that Judas was the only Apostle who was a Judean. All the others were from Galilee. The term "Iscariot" was probably given to him to distinguish him from the other Judas among the Apostles; Judas son of James (Acts 1:13; John 14:22).
- Talented: He was handpicked, as all the apostles were. Jesus saw in him great potential and talent. He was certainly a man of some administration skills as Jesus gave to him the responsibility of caring for the group's financial needs (John 13:29). As funds came and went, it was all under Judas' management. As such, he was no doubt given some degree of respect from the less financially astute Galileans.

- Tempted: Over time he became a thief. The somewhat significant funds necessary to sustain a group of twelve began to tempt him, and at some point he crossed the line and began to steal from these funds (John 12:6). He became a common thief. Like all thieves, when caught, he took whatever steps necessary to cover up his theft.
- Destroyed: After his betrayal his life spun out of control. Allowing Satan to enter his heart, his guilty conscience led him to the taking of his own life (Matthew 27:3-5).

The Points:

His Betrayal: When Judas walked into the Judgment Hall of the High Priest and began to bargain over money and betrayal, he entered into a partnership with a group of men who were interested in only one thing - the death of Jesus of Nazareth. It is clear that he rationalized his own actions. Jesus had discovered his stealing, and he needed to get rid of the one man who could bring justice down upon him. With Jesus' arrest, Judas perhaps thought he could make his escape, get away with the money he had in the bag, and add to it the thirty pieces of silver.

The text of John 12:4-8 makes it clear that Jesus was aware of his actions. Realizing that he had been caught red-handed, he sought to protect himself. All thieves are selfish and care little for their victims. The depths of his actions, however, at last caught up with him, and lost in the guilt of his betrayal, he tried desperately to undo the wrong he had done. His attempt to cleanse his soul by returning the money was rejected, and he could only hurl the coins at the dreadful men with whom he had partnered. When Judas left the upper room we are told, "and it was night" (John 13:30). How dark that night must have been!

His Love of Money: The story of Judas is the classic example of the path of destruction that the love of money will take all who fall into its trap. How could you fill your own pocket with the Lord's money? How could you accept coins from the temple treasury to betray the Messiah? Oh the depths to which this love will take a man's soul!

His Impenitent Spirit: Judas' greatest character flaw was not his thievery, but his proud spirit. Jesus had many disciples that made mistakes that disappointed him and who gave in to Satan's temptations. We need to look no further than Peter to see another Apostle who stumbled and failed often in the Lord's service. Yet Peter and many others were quick to recognize their faults, and Jesus was just as quick to forgive and work with them to overcome them. Had Judas fallen at Jesus' feet and asked his forgiveness, do we think for a moment that Jesus would not forgive him as he had others? But Judas was not interested in forgiveness. Instead he sought revenge, and sought to cash in. This was his real downfall. As Jesus said, "unless you repent, you will all likewise perish" (Luke 13:3). And perish Judas did by his own hand.

What Do You Think?

1. In our world today how does the "love of money" continue to destroy lives? Look at Paul's teaching in 1 Timothy 6:6-10. Jesus and his ministry needed money for food and other travel expenses, and in the end to buy necessary items for the Passover. Money was necessary and was used for good. How does necessity turn into love?

2. Most criminals only express sorrow after they are caught. Most of the time when they say they are sorry, it only means that they are sorry that they got caught. Was this the case for Judas? Why are some people so unwilling to repent?

3. What do you think it means when we are told that the devil put into the heart of Judas the act of betrayal (John 13:2)? Was Judas an innocent victim?

Lesson Eight
"The Bread and the Body"
Read Section Three, Chapter 5
Read Matthew 26:26-30; Mark 14:26-31; Luke 22:17-20

The Facts:

Do we understand the heritage of this "unleavened bread?" Each Lord's Day when we break the bread, do we really understand its symbolism? What is Jesus asking of us today as we partake of this sacred bread?

The first account of unleavened bread is Genesis 19:3. Lot persuaded the two angels to stay with him in his home and he fixed them unleavened bread. Since he was not expecting them, they had no time to bake leavened bread. Here we see that unleavened bread was the bread of haste (Exodus 12:11).

As Moses gave the instructions for that first Passover in Egypt, he told them that they were to prepare "unleavened bread" with the lamb (Exodus 12:8). This same bread was then commanded to be eaten in the yearly observances of the Passover.

The Passover was a week long celebration often called the "feast of unleavened bread." On the first day, all leaven was to be removed from the home (Exodus 12:14-15). Later tradition added that anything that had touched any leaven was to be thoroughly washed.

Unleavened bread was eaten on the day of their deliverance from Egypt and always beenconnected to that great event. "Moses said to the people, 'Remember this day in which you went out from Egypt, from the house of slavery, for by a powerful hand the Lord brought you out from this place. And nothing leavened shall be eaten'" (Exodus 13:3).

The Points:

<u>Unleavened Bread Then:</u> When Jesus reclined at the Passover table, the sacrificed lamb was there, as was the prescribed unleavened bread. This was by the commandment of the Scriptures we have noted above. The unleavened bread represented in the Passover the deliverance of God's people from bondage in Egypt. As Jesus broke it in the upper room, he clearly gave a new meaning to it. It was in this manner that Jesus taught that this was the final Passover to be celebrated. The "new" memorial meal would be partaken of with them "in my Father's Kingdom" (Matthew 26:29).

<u>Unleavened Bread Today:</u> There is no direct command in the New Testament for us to use unleavened bread in the Lord's Supper. When Jesus broke the bread in the Upper Room the text does not directly use the term "unleavened bread." Two points: First, by law and tradition the bread used by the Jews in this celebration in Christ's day was unleavened bread. Today the Jews still use unleavened bread in their modern observance of the Passover. Second, it is our desire to look to the scriptures and to copy or duplicate the actions of Christ and his church as much as we can. Since we know that the bread that Jesus broke in the upper room was unleavened bread, we too use unleavened bread. The implication of 1 Corinthians 5:6-9 is that the New Testament church continued to use unleavened bread in the Lord's Supper.

The Meaning of the Bread: Jesus gave a new meaning to the bread. As He broke it he said, "this is my body which is given for you; do this in remembrance of Me" (Luke 22:19). The bread of the Lord's Supper represents the physical body, the physical suffering, the physical death that Jesus endured. Jesus came into this world in a physical way, through the womb, "born of a woman" (Galatians 4:4). God "became flesh and dwelt among us" (John 1:14). Jesus grew from a babe, to a child, to a man. He hungered and became thirsty, he cried real tears, he bled real blood, and he felt strong emotional as well as physical pain. He gave this physical body to be scourged and suffered that agonizing death in that body on the cross. When we break the bread, we remember the physical and emotional sufferings of Jesus on the cross.

What Do You Think?

1. Paul said in Romans that we as Gentiles were "grafted" into the vine (Romans 11:17-22). How does unleavened bread connect us to the roots, or vine, of the old Law?
2. How does this study make the breaking of the bread more meaningful to you? Do we sometimes break the bread with little thought to its meaning? If so, how can we change that?
3. In the Garden of Gethsemane we see the emotional pain Jesus was suffering. On the cross we see the physical pain he endured. How do we connect to that in the breaking of the bread?

Lesson Nine
"The Cup and the Blood"
Read Section Three, Chapter 5
*Read Mark 14:22-25; Hebrews 9:22, 10:10-12;
1 Corinthians 11:25*

The Facts:

The breaking of the bread represented Christ's physical sufferings. He took the cup and told his Apostles that this drink, this "fruit of the vine" was to represent his blood given for a new covenant. This is a very dramatic moment in the upper room, and a symbolic action that we must come to understand in order to do this each week in remembrance of Him.

- The cup of wine mentioned in the upper room was not a part of the original observance of the Passover. We do not read of wine in the first Passover in Egypt or in subsequent directions in the old Law. The addition of the "cup" occurred in that period between the testaments and was added to represent the festive side of the Passover celebration.

- The contents of the cup was revealed to us by Christ; he said it was "fruit of the vine." This would have been grape juice, either freshly prepared (new wine) or some which had been stored in wine skins (old wine). Compare Luke 5:37.

- There were three, and later four, blessings offered during the Passover, each involving a cup of wine. Much like we might offer up a toast at a wedding, these "cups" were offered up at appropriate times by the host.

- It was traditional for the host to offer up the first toast, or "cup," to begin the Passover meal, at which time the host would remind those around the table of how God brought his people out of Egypt. Jesus broke with that tradition by offering the first cup and proclaiming the coming of God's kingdom. He stated, "I shall never again eat it until it is fulfilled in the kingdom of God" (Luke 22:15-17). Luke is the only Gospel writer to inform us of Jesus' words during the offering of this first cup.
- It was at the occasion of the second cup, after he had broken the bread, that Jesus offered new meaning to the cup of wine, "This is my blood of the covenant, which is poured out for many" (Mark 14:24).

The Points:

The End of the Jewish Passover: After breaking the bread and offering the cup Jesus said "I will never again drink of the fruit of the vine until that day when I drink it new in the kingdom of God" (Mark 14:25) This is a significant statement. Jesus is saying that he and his Apostles will not be eating the Passover again. The next time the "fruit of the vine" is drunk in a memorial meal, it will be new, observed not under Mosaic law, but in the new kingdom!

Jesus nailed the old Law to the cross, which did away with "decrees" such as animal sacrifices, feast days, and the Passover (Colossians 2:14).

We now have a better sacrifice (Hebrews 10:11-12) a better priest (Hebrews 7:23-24) and a better covenant (Hebrews 8:6). We also have a new memorial meal to go with this new covenant.

The Meaning of the Cup: Jesus offered the cup, which was filled with wine, and said, "This is my blood of the covenant, which is poured out for many for the forgiveness of sins" (Matthew 26:28). While the bread represents what Jesus did for us physically in offering up his body, the wine represents the blood of Jesus which did something amazing for us spiritually. Jesus' blood forgave all sins past, present, and future! He said at that table that it was "for the forgiveness of sins." Through his own blood he forgave sins "once for all" (Hebrews 9:12). Remember that under the Law of Moses there was no forgiveness of sins. "For it is impossible for the blood of bulls and goats to take away sins" (Hebrews 10:4). The cup which we partake of around the Lord's Table is symbolic of that blood.

No Forgiveness in the Cup: The "fruit of the vine" that we drink does not take away sins. It is an action of remembrance until the Lord returns. The power of the blood to forgive sins is released in the waters of baptism, not in the wine of the cup. When a lamb was sacrificed in the temple, the blood was sprinkled around the altar. Jesus is our Lamb and we read that our "hearts were sprinkled clean" with the blood of Jesus and our bodies were "washed with pure water" (Hebrews 10:19-23). Forgiveness takes place in the blood and the water. See also Romans 6:1-6 and Acts 22:16.

What Do You Think?

1. What made Jesus' blood so special? What gave it the power to forgive our sins?
2. The writer of Hebrews said that Jesus was the "propitiation" for our sins (Hebrews 2:17 NKJV, NASB). What does the word "propitiation" mean? What does it tell us about the blood of Jesus?
3. Are Christians still under the Ten Commandments? Why or why not?

Lesson Ten
Jesus' After Dinner Speeches
Read Section Three, Chapter 6
Read John 14 – 17

The Facts:

- As the Passover dinner came to an end, a foreboding stillness must have filled the room. The Passover meal was traditionally a festive time, a meal to celebrate a great event in their nation's history, a joyous family time. But the mood of the Savior, the scene of him washing feet, the betrayal talk and departure of Judas, and finally his words spoken over the bread and the cup of his broken body and shed blood, all created an atmosphere of gloom, confusion, and despair.

- After dinner speeches are usually meant to be light-hearted and uplifting. As Jesus began to speak at the conclusion of the meal, his words were not jovial by any means, but they were meant to be encouraging and informative. He began with the famous words, "Let not your heart be troubled." Jesus made it clear that although he would leave them, he would be returning. He then encouraged them by letting them know that a comforter would be with them while he was gone. He exhorted them to love one another, and assured them that the Father loved them as well. His speech surely lifted their spirits.

- Part of Jesus' speech was probably given as they walked from the upper room, down the deserted city streets and into the moonlight of the Kidron valley. We know at some point they sang a song and left the upper room (Matthew 26:30). Jesus knew that Judas would soon be on his way, and he longed for the solitude of Gethsemane. So he surely spoke as they walked along, perhaps stopping along the way to emphasize important points and engage in some discussions. At the end of John 14 Jesus said, "Get up, let us go from here." This was the point when they left the upper room. The words of John 15 and 16 were most likely given during their journey to Gethsemane. His prayer to his Father in John 17, perhaps with his Apostles gathered around him under the stars of heaven, brought his messages to a close.

The Points:

<u>His Father's House: John 14:1-3</u> The opening verses of John 14 are some of the most famous Jesus ever spoke. In these words He gives us a unique insight into what our afterlife will be like. He says, depending upon your translation, "in my Father's house are many rooms/dwelling places/mansions." The word in question here is the Greek word mone; it means, "a state of remaining in an area, staying, tarrying." Jesus' comment is not about a structure, but about a location; his "Father's house." Jesus was telling his disciples, and teaching us, that in his Father's living quarters there is plenty of room for each of us to come stay. Heaven will be being in the very presence of God! Jesus further emphasizes this point when he says, "That where I am there you may be also" (John 14:3). Heaven is about being with Christ, being with God, being with all the saints; how wonderful that will be!

The Spirit of Truth: John 14:16-18; 16:13-16 Jesus had much to say about his impending departure from them, but then assured them that he would not leave them "orphans." Jesus knew that his work would soon be done; then it would be the Holy Spirit that would guide, inspire, and comfort these men. The Spirit did come upon them on the day of Pentecost (Acts 2:1-4) and continued to guide them in what to teach (Acts 2:42) and to give them the courage to defend the truth (Acts 4:13).

Abide in Me: John 15:1-8 Some of these men would be tempted to leave the group. Jesus encouraged them, "I am the vine, you are the branches;" "Abide in me;" "Bear much fruit." What wonderful words of encouragement! Many Christians today become discouraged and do leave the Lord's vineyard. How tragic! For those of us who stay, let us be reminded of our responsibility to bear fruit. We need to go out into our communities and be that salt of the earth, to be that candle that gives light to all, to show people our faith by our works, and in so doing to win others to the Lord.

The Power of Prayer: John 16:23-28 Jesus let these men know that after he was gone, they could communicate with the Father through him. He gave them great confidence by letting them know that any need that they had, all they needed to do was to ask in his name, and they would receive it. Whatever they needed to "go into all the world," if they would but ask, it would be granted to them. What a powerful resource prayer is!

What Do You Think?

1. In what ways has the term "mansions" distorted our view of heaven? What are some of your thoughts about what it will be like to be in the very presence of God?
2. Besides guiding the Apostles in those early days of the church, what other ways was the Spirit active? See Acts 2:38; Acts 8:29; 2 Peter 1:20-21.
3. Are we a prayerful people? Do you believe that there were some things that happened because you prayed, that would not have happened if you had not prayed? Are there things that could have happened, that did not happen, because you failed to pray?

Lesson Eleven
"The Failings of the Pharisees"
Read Section Two, Chapters 8 and 10
Read Matthew 23

The Facts:

- The Pharisees were a religious and political party under Judaism. Their roots went back to the Hasidim party and the revolt of the Maccabees against the Hellenist Jews in the second century B.C. Hellenist Jews followed very few Jewish customs and lived much like their Gentile neighbors. The Hasidim insisted on strict observance of Jewish ritual laws.

- In fierce battles Judas Maccabaeus and the Hasidim party overthrew the Hellenist's control of Jerusalem and the temple. After their victory they restored and rededicated the temple. The Jews celebrated this every year. It was called the "feast of Lights" or the "feast of Dedication" and was observed by Christ in John 10:22-23. The Jews continue to celebrate this event today under the name of "Hanukkah," which comes from the Hebrew word meaning, "to dedicate."

- Afterwards, the Hasidim party split; one group withdrew from society, formed their own communities, and became known as the Essenes. It is likely that it was a group of Essenes that lived in Qumran and gave us the Dead Sea Scrolls. The other group became the Pharisees, an important and powerful force in Jewish life.

- The Pharisees became known for insisting that the Law of Moses be strictly observed as the scribes interpreted it. They had their own special traditions of keeping the law. Many of the priests, scribes, and members of the Sanhedrin were Pharisees, as was Paul the Apostle in his earlier days (Acts 26:5). There was another religious party in the majority in Jesus' day, known as the Sadducees. They were less zealous in keeping the law, and did not believe in things such as the resurrection and angels. They gave little attention to Jesus, while the Pharisees led in the attacks and eventual murder of Jesus.

The Points:

<u>The Pharisees studied and taught the Law;</u> Before his condemnation of them, Jesus praised the Pharisees by saying, "The scribes and the Pharisees have seated themselves in the chair of Moses; therefore all that they tell you, do and observe" (Matthew 23:2-3). Before we condemn the Pharisees, let us first achieve their respect and study of God's Word. Jesus said to them, "You search the scriptures because you think that in them you have eternal life. It is these that testify of me" (John 5:39). Let us today be students of the Word and spend time in "searching the Scriptures." Let us be capable teachers ready to show others the way of the Lord. On the other hand, the problem with the Pharisees was that they gave attention to little things to the neglect of the "weightier provisions of the law" (Matthew 23:23).

The world's biggest hypocrites: The Pharisees were the very essence of hypocrisy. It was the single biggest accusation of the Lord against them. On the outside they were one thing, on the inside they were something else. "First clean the inside of the cup and of the dish, so that the outside of it may become clean also" (Matthew 23:26). This hypocrisy made them feel like they were better than others. It was the Pharisee that Jesus said went up to the temple to pray and thanked God that "I am not like other people: swindlers, unjust, adulterers, or even like this tax collector" (Luke 18:11). It is for this reason that their biggest complaint against Jesus was that he ate with tax collectors and sinners. The Pharisees were egotistical, stuck-up, power-hungry men.

The Pharisees let their traditions override the Scriptures: They asked Jesus, "Why do your disciples break the tradition of the elders? For they do not wash their hands when they eat bread." Jesus' response was, "Why do you yourselves transgress the commandment of God for the sake of your tradition?" He then gave the example of support of their parents and said, "But in vain do they worship me, teaching as doctrines the precepts of men" (Matthew 15:1-9). No Scripture was so important that it could not be overridden by their traditions.

What Do You Think?

1. How would you describe your study of the Bible - every week at home, every day, only when I am at church? How does study of the Scriptures affect the growth of your faith?

2. As Christians do we have to guard against hypocrisy? Do we leave the impression sometimes that we are better than some poor person that we do not want to help, or teach, or sit next to? Do we look down our noses at some bad sinner and not want them to attend our services?

3. Do we have traditions in our churches that we hold as sacred? Are we unwilling to change our worship time, our song service, and/or order because of our traditions? How do the traditions of men show up in other religious groups?

Lesson Twelve
"A Cup of Tea at Calvary"

Read Section One, Chapter 1 and Section Three, Epilogue

Read 1 Corinthians 11:23-32

The Facts:

- History of Crucifixion: In the Old Testament, there were those who were executed by stoning, their bodies were often put on public display by hanging them on a tree. But the law commanded that the body be taken down by sundown and buried (Deuteronomy 21:23). The Greeks were the first to use crucifixion as a main means to execute their enemies. Alexander the Great hung two thousand people on crosses when he captured the city of Tyre. The Romans developed crucifixion to a science, using it to execute their enemies in a humiliating and painful fashion. Roman soldiers could keep a man alive on a cross and in agonizing pain for many days before he died. Crucifixion continued to be used until Emperor Constantine converted to Christianity and ended it, turning the cross into a symbol of Christianity.
- Shape of the Cross: There were four different shapes of crosses used in Jesus' day. The Latin cross, shaped like a lower case "t", on which it seems likely that Jesus died, because of the notice placed above his head (Matthew 27:37); The St. Anthony cross, which was shaped like a capital "T"; the St. Andrew cross in the shape of an "X"; and the Greek cross which had the cross beam in the center like a plus sign.

- Golgotha: The place where Jesus was crucified, an Aramaic word meaning "Place of the skull" (Mark 15:22). The Latin Vulgate translation used the Latin word "calvaria" from which we get our English word "Calvary." The location was most likely just outside the city walls of Jerusalem in a place near public travel. Today there are two possible sights offered, the Catholic sight at the Church of the Holy Sepulcher, and "Gordon's Calvary" outside the present wall of the city and near the famous garden tomb.

The Points:

Proclaiming the Lord's Death: The Apostle Paul, in teaching the church in Corinth about the proper manner in which to take the Lord's Supper said, "For as often as you eat this bread, and drink this cup, you proclaim the Lord's death until he comes" (1 Corinthians 11:26). We break this bread so that we, our children and grandchildren, and the world, will never forget Jesus' death on the cross and all of its meaning. When we break the bread, we make a "proclamation" to all that Jesus died for us, and we will never forget his sacrifice!

Our Worship: We see in the events of the upper room those items which are the essential ingredients of our present worship; in Jesus' washing of feet we learn that we are to come around the table as humble servants and in love of one another. In the breaking of the bread and drinking of the cup, we remember the Lord's death on the cross for us. In blessing the same, we pray to our Father, whom we praise in song as the Apostles did in their closing. In Jesus' teachings in the upper room, we see the need to preach and study God's Word. The Lord's Supper is not only a part of our worship, but as we can see, it is our worship! All that we do on the first day of the week is centered around the Lord's Table.

That Cup of Tea: Many years ago my dearest friend from college and I took a trip to Israel on our own. We arrived at Tel Aviv in the middle of the night and joined some other men in a taxi trip up to Jerusalem. We had the driver let my friend and I out near the old city. It was around 4:00 in the morning and a heavy mist or fog had engulfed the city. It was an eerie scene. We dropped our bags off at a small local hotel and began to wander around looking for a place to get something to eat.

We found a man opening his shop and asked him if we could get some food. He motioned to us to follow him down the side of his building and around to the back. We followed. I could tell as we walked that there was an empty field next to the building. He had us sit on some crates and went inside, emerging shortly with some hot tea and pastries. We enjoyed our refreshments as the sun began to rise over the old city of Jerusalem. As the fog slowly began to lift, I could see what was across the field and realized it was the bus station. I had been to Jerusalem a few years before and suddenly realized where we were. I turned behind me and found myself staring up at the hill known as Gordon's Calvary. We were having a cup of tea at the foot of Calvary. It was a surreal moment, one I would never forget, and one that I have called to memory many times on Sunday mornings as I partook of the Lord's Supper.

It is my hope that this book, and these lessons, have helped bring you to the foot of Calvary, to Golgotha's cruel site, with a better understanding of how Jesus came to be on that cross. In so doing, perhaps your remembrance of his sacrifice as you gather around the Lord's Table every first day of the week will be enriched.

What Do You Think?

1. How was Jesus' execution different from the kind of executions we see in the United States of America? How is the intent of the executions different?

2. How do you prepare yourself spiritually and mentally to partake the Lord's Supper? What way does the worship itself give importance to the Lord's Supper? What do you do or think during those moments the bread and cup are passed? How well do you think most Christians truly remember the Lord's death during these moments?

3. How can we partake in "an unworthy manner"? When Paul asks us to "examine ourselves," he is talking about examining how we are partaking of this memorial meal. Are we remembering? Are we proclaiming?

Bibliography

Broadhurst, Donna, and Mal Broadhurst. *Passover: Before Messiah and After.* Carol Stream, IL: Shofar Publications, 1987.

Coffman, James Burton. *Commentary on the Gospel of Matthew.* Austin, TX: Firm Foundation Publishing, 1979.

The Daily Bible in Chronological Order, NIV. Eugene, OR: Harvest House Publishers, 1973.

Edersheim, Alfred. *The Life and Times of Jesus the Messiah.* MacLean, VA: MacDonald Publishing, 1983.

Edersheim, Alfred. *The Temple: Its Ministry and Services as They Were at the Time of Jesus Christ, Updated Edition.* Peabody, MA: Hendrickson Publishers, Inc., 1994.

Farrar, Frederic W. *The Life of Christ.* Portland, OR: Fountain Publications, 1972.

Hendriksen, William, and Simon Kistemaker. *New Testament Commentary.* Grand Rapids, MI: Baker Book House, 2002.

The Holy Bible, English Standard Version. Wheaton: Crossway Bibles, 2008.

The Holy Bible, New Iinternational Version. Grand Rapids: Zondervan Publishing House, 1984.

Kyle, Melvin Grove, and James Orr. *International Standard Bible Encyclopeida.* Grand Rapids, MI: W. B. Eerdmans Publishing Co., 1956.

New American Standard Bible. La Habra, CA: The Lockman Foundation, 1995.

The New English Bible. Oxford: Oxford University Press, 1970.

Peterson, Eugene H. *The Message.* Colorado Springs: Nav Press Publishing Group, 2003.

Robertson, A. T. *A Harmony of the Gospels for Students of the Life of Christ.* New York: Harper and Row Publishers, 1922.

Singer, Isidore, and Cyrus Adler. *The Jewish Encyclopedia : a descriptive record of the history, religion, literature, and customs of the Jewish people from the earliest times to the present day.* KTAV Publishing House, 1900.

Thomas, Robert L. and Stanley N. Gundry. *The NIV Harmony of the Gospels.* San Francisco: Harper and Row Publishers, 1988.

Vincent, Marvin Richardson. *Word Studies in the New Testament.* Wilmington, DE: Associated Publishers and Authors, 1972.

Youngblood, Ronald F., ed. *Nelson's New Illustrated Bible Dictionary.* Nashville: Thomas Nelson Publishers, 1995.

www.ingramcontent.com/pod-product-compliance
Lightning Source LLC
Chambersburg PA
CBHW060508100426
42743CB00009B/1260